FIELD & FEAST

Sublime Food from a Brave New Farm

DEAN CARLSON
with Ian Knauer and Andrew Wood

PHOTOGRAPHS BY GUY AMBROSINO

BLP
BURGESS LEA PRESS

CONTENTS

HERB
GARDEN

INTRODUCTION

A Part of Something Bigger *by Dean Carlson*

The road to Wyebrook Farm winds through the rolling countryside of southeastern Pennsylvania. It runs across a bridge over a brook, then alongside a long stone wall. The wall was built by laborers from the nearby Isabella Furnace, an anthracite coal–powered iron furnace that last operated in 1894. It must have taken years to clear those stones from the fields. Fieldstones also form the foundations of the barn and the houses on the property.

As you turn onto the lane that leads to the heart of our farm, fields stretch before you until they disappear into the horizon to the right and flow into a tree line far down the hill on the left. After a few hundred yards, a wooded curve in the lane brings the houses and barn into view. In summer, the field grass sways back and forth like waves.

Wyebrook came to me with its name. In 1906, a local writer named Wilmer W. MacElree waxed on about the shape of the letter Y as he traveled to the farm's namesake brook. With its gently sloping fields and fresh running water, the place lends itself perfectly to being farmed, which is exactly what has been happening here for more than 200 years.

A few years ago, I was the least likely person in the world to become a farmer. I had studied economics and spent my professional life working as a derivatives and bond trader. During the financial crisis in 2009, I took some time off from work. I planned to read, surf, and travel, then return to the market when things were looking better. But then I read *The Omnivore's Dilemma*.

People with my background tend not to go into farming for lots of reasons, but front and center is the simple fact that the way we farm now is just not economically viable. All of our economic models are based on the idea that as demand increases, supply will always rise to meet it. They do not take into account the fact that the supply of some inputs is finite. The assumption of continuous economic growth always troubled me on some level, but after reading Michael Pollan's groundbreaking book and coming to understand the implications of exponential growth, my life's path changed completely.

In the book, Pollan reports that our way of farming requires 57 fossil fuel calories to produce just one food calorie. You don't have to be a student of economics to find this statistic shocking. We rely—heavily—on a finite resource to produce our food. No matter your thoughts on when that resource will run out, it will run out. Once you consider other facts—for instance, human population growth and our ever-increasing need for food—the situation starts to seem dire. Yet very little has been done to avoid what will certainly be a global disaster.

I believe that the end of cheap fossil fuels is upon us and that we have very little time to make some gigantic changes. And while our world will be profoundly different when we can no longer rely on cheap fossil fuel, we can live without it. We cannot live without food.

It is astounding how much energy is used to get food on the table. Sure, tractors use diesel, but that's only the tip of the iceberg. The fertilizers applied to the majority of farmland in this country are produced from natural gas. An enormous amount of fuel is used to ship food. Much of the beef we eat in the U.S. is shipped in from Argentina and beyond. These ways of farming and delivering food are not sustainable. Moreover, they're not necessary.

The notion that we urgently need to find new, sustainable ways to produce our food affected me so deeply that I started looking for farmland to buy. When I found Wyebrook, the 320-acre farm was in disrepair and bank-owned, which was a large part of the appeal. I would have felt out of my league at an auction, and even less comfortable offering to purchase a farm that had been in a family for generations, as is the case with much of the nearby farmland. But the bank wanted to get it off their hands and off their books. They would have had no qualms selling to a housing developer or a commercial builder. I'm glad I was able to buy Wyebrook and continue its tradition of farming.

I spent the first several months cleaning up junk everywhere. There was a huge crack in the barn wall and the roof needed replacing. The floorboards did, too. I spent hours with architects figuring out how to build a modern commercial kitchen in a building designed to house workhorses. My goal was not just to build a sustainable farm, but to create a welcoming space where the community could gather, eat, and buy their food locally. On the farm,

animals would spend every day of their lives, including their last, in a healthy environment, and I envisioned a restaurant and market that would treat the meat from those animals with the respect they deserve. When all those steps happen in one location, we start to streamline food production in a natural way, removing much of the need for fossil fuels. Just as important, we have a closer relationship to, and deeper respect for, the meat we eat.

I aim to make Wyebrook energy independent. We're not there yet, but much of what we do reverts back to practices from times past. The farm is primarily run on solar energy, and while there are panels on the barn roofs that capture sunlight and convert it into electricity, that's not the only kind of solar energy I'm referring to. I mean the sun that grows the grass, the grass that converts that energy into chlorophyll, and the cattle that harvest the grass themselves—getting rid of the need for gas-powered equipment—and convert that chlorophyll into protein and fat.

Sustainable farming sets out to produce food in a way that can be repeated infinitely on a given piece of land. A grass-based system uses inputs that can be renewed year after year. Because grass is a perennial plant, it does not have to be tilled. In fact, as the animals graze, the soil becomes better over time as they provide an evenly distributed layer of fertilizer back to the earth. Sustainable farming simply tries to find ways to mimic systems found in nature and improve upon them.

Cattle and sheep are herbivores and so only require grass to grow. Pigs and chickens need grain, but the production of grain is incredibly energy intensive and highly correlated with fossil fuel prices. Again, I look for ways in which nature would have provided for these animals. Wild pigs will root and forage along the forest floor. So I planted several hundred trees in and around our pastures for shade, water retention, and as a food source. I partially logged some of the forested areas to create savannahs so that grass can grow on the forest floor, but saved all the mast producing trees as a food source for the pigs. Feeding animals this way will become more and more important as the cost of grain rises with oil prices.

This kind of farming is better on every level of the food chain. Soil microbes benefit from the natural fertilizer dropped on them from the grazing animals, as well as from the elimination of plowing and tilling. The grasses and mast trees (those that produce acorns or nuts) benefit from that healthy soil. The animals get to spend their lives mostly outside and eat a diet that is considerably healthier for them than grain. And finally, humans benefit from eating meat free from disease and chemicals.

We can make these changes willingly now or have them forced upon us at some point in the future. When you purchase local, sustainably raised food, you contribute to changing our food system, and the impact of our collective decision can be incredibly powerful. If Wyebrook's customers feel like they are a part of something bigger, it's because they are. They all choose to spend their food dollars in a way that can make a difference. And there is community inherent in that. We are all in it together to eat better and to live better.

Chef Dinner with Ian
Saturday May 12th, 2014
Chef Ian Knauer

WHO'S WHO AT WYEBROOK FARM

DEAN AND EMELIE CARLSON

The Visionaries

Dean and Emelie Carlson live and work at Wyebrook, he with his soft-spoken, Midwestern demeanor, she with her Scandinavian sense of style and subtlety. After 15 years on Wall Street, Dean rolled up his sleeves and dove into what he calls a "real job." He is present for every step of the farming process, and the circle of sustainability he is creating informs his every decision. His quiet ways are balanced with Emelie's natural joie de vivre. They were married on the farm, and their family—including newborn son Sven and Dean's daughter Emmie—is the trunk from which the Wyebrook community sprouts.

RYAN BOSTDORF

The Farmer

Ryan Bostdorf is a man of the animals. He has lived around them and studied them for most of his life. Without his expertise in animal welfare and grass-based systems, there would be no dinner at the farm. Ryan spends his days (and some nights) with the pigs, cattle, chickens, goats, sheep and any other animal nearby including his dog, who is constantly by his side, helping to herd the pigs and cattle, and wearing a wide smile all the time.

ALEXI ALEJANDRO

The Butcher

Every serving of meat at Wyebrook, from the thinly sliced smoked shoulder of beef in the café's sandwich to the pork belly with spring nettles, passes through the careful hands and sharp knife of Alexi Alejandro. His craft is to disassemble the mosaic of muscle before him and fill both the kitchen and the market with steaks, chops, offal, and more. Nothing is wasted. Alexi's youth and expertise are mismatched. His innate understanding of butchery is a gift. He's discovered he was born to do exactly this.

BRYAN MAYER

The Mentor

Bryan Mayer has dedicated his life to practice, learning, and teaching—first through music, now through thoughtful butchering of sustainably raised meat. He chops, saws and slices with finesse, and understands that the animals raised at Wyebrook Farm deserve our respect. Bryan's deep familiarity with the rituals and realities of butchery is indispensable when he leads our pig slaughter at La Tuade in the fall.

ANDREW WOOD

The Chef

Andrew Wood has an encyclopedic depth of knowledge in both French and Italian technique, but also the ability to reinvent classics, using hyper-local ingredients to assign them a new sense of place—in this case, the eastern Pennsylvania countryside. His sensibility of provenance is most easily seen through his food. The ingredients come from here and are either used fresh or preserved throughout the year. Andrew's perspective on food is based on the relationships he has developed with farmers, the seasons, and life itself.

MATT BROEZE

The Cook

Matt Broeze is the muscle, mind, and watchful eyes of the kitchen. As Wyebrook's chef de cuisine, he's the guy who runs the daily operations—a job that requires skill, careful organization, and constant energy. It's a perfect position for someone who cannot sit still. Matt came to the farm after stints at some of the area's most celebrated restaurants, including Andrew's own Russet in Philadelphia. He uses his top-notch training to craft the most memorable meals.

IAN KNAUER

The Wordsmith

Ian Knauer has spent his career as a cook, writer, and teacher who revels in working with the freshest ingredients. After eating his way around the world, he realized that our eastern Pennsylvania food traditions can be considered world class cuisine. He's on a mission to prove that to anyone who will listen or taste. Long-time farmers, the Knauer family has been a neighbor to Wyebrook since before the place was named, and Ian knows this land and its ways well.

PORK

The Other Red Meat

In the past, pigs were raised primarily for their ability to produce a large amount of fat. Lard was prized in the kitchen, as other cooking fats were relatively hard to come by. The introduction of hydrogenated vegetable oils caused lard to fall out of favor, and pork marketers came up with the gimmick of "the other white meat." As pigs began to be bred for leaner meat, their fat—and subsequently, their flavor—was lost.

We raise heritage breed pigs because they are full of that once-prized intramuscular fat, which protects the meat from drying out during cooking and adds plenty of umami. We happily use any extra fat in our kitchen and as charcuterie. Equally important, most heritage breeds are accustomed to spending their lives on pasture instead of being crammed together inside a feedlot. Many of the modern breeds simply are not hardy enough to live outside.

We raise Berkshire, Gloucestershire Old Spots, and Tamworth hogs, all of which are registered as rare breeds in England and produce large amounts of fat. In addition, we keep Chester Whites, which have been bred here in Chester County since the mid-1800s, and Ossabaws.

The Ossabaw has a wonderful history. In the 1500s, the Spanish dropped hardy pigs on Ossabaw Island, Georgia, intending to use them as a future food source. The animals thrived, feral on the island, until they were captured and bred in the 1980s. This particular breed looks more like a wild boar than a domestic pig, and, not surprisingly, they are terrific foragers. Ossabaws have the ability to transform a relatively small amount of food into a huge amount of fat.

The meat of the Ossabaw is extraordinary—dark red with a rich, deep flavor very different from the pork we have grown accustomed to eating in the last several decades. The problem with the Ossabaws, from a production standpoint, is that they grow very slowly, have small loins, and produce small litters. Because of this, it's unlikely they will ever be widely adopted in the modern food system. That's too bad. If more Americans were to taste the Ossabaw, I don't think we'd ever go back to that other white meat. *—Dean*

SALT CRUST–BAKED PORK BELLY
with Hickory Nut Romesco

Hickory trees dot the eastern Pennsylvania forests and drop their sweet, oily nuts in the early autumn, when our pigs happily forage them. This dish lets us serve the nuts, in a savory romesco sauce, with our hickory-fed pork. It might seem excessive to brine a piece of meat overnight and then bake it in a salt crust, but worry not—the result is a moist, perfectly seasoned pork belly.

SERVES 6 TO 8

FOR THE PORK BELLY

1 (3-pound) piece fresh pork belly, skin removed

4 cups Heavy Brine (page 249)

6 cups coarse sea salt

¾ cup all-purpose flour

1 cup water

12 garlic cloves, sliced

2 bunches fresh thyme

2 bunches fresh sage

1 large bunch parsley

½ cup Dehydrated Sweet Peppers (page 239), crushed to a powder

FOR THE SAUCE

3 red bell peppers, halved and seeded

⅓ cup plus ¼ cup extra-virgin olive oil

1 (1-inch-thick) slice sourdough bread, torn into small pieces

½ cup hickory nuts or hazelnuts

6 garlic cloves, smashed

1 tablespoon smoked paprika

2 cups Roasted Tomato Purée (page 230)

Fine sea salt

1 to 2 tablespoons red wine vinegar

For the pork belly: Place the pork belly in the brine and refrigerate overnight.

Preheat the oven to 450°F. Line an 8 x 11-inch roasting pan with aluminum foil.

Remove the pork belly from the brine and pat dry. In a large bowl, stir together the salt, flour, and water until well combined. Spread a thin layer of the salt mixture over the bottom of the lined roasting pan. Scatter half of the garlic, thyme, sage, and parsley over the salt then place the pork belly over the herb layer. Sprinkle the crushed dehydrated sweet peppers over the pork, followed by the remaining garlic and herbs. Pack the remaining salt mixture over and around the pork belly.

Roast the pork belly until the salt crust is well browned, about 2½ hours. Let the pork belly cool in the salt crust for 1 hour.

While the pork belly roasts, make the romesco sauce: Grill or broil the peppers until their skins are blackened, about 15 minutes. Transfer the peppers to a paper bag, fold the bag closed, and let stand for 10 minutes. Slip off and discard the skins; reserve the peppers.

Heat ⅓ cup of the olive oil in a large heavy skillet over medium-high heat until hot. Add the bread and nuts and fry, stirring frequently, until golden, about 5 minutes. Stir in the garlic and cook until golden, about 2 minutes. Add the paprika and cook, stirring, until fragrant, about 30 seconds. Add the tomato purée and ½ teaspoon salt and boil, stirring occasionally, until the mixture thickens, about 6 minutes. Transfer the mixture to a blender, and add the reserved peppers. With the motor running, pour the remaining ¼ cup oil into the sauce and blend until smooth. Season to taste with salt and the vinegar. (The romesco sauce keeps, refrigerated in an airtight container, for 2 weeks.)

To serve, preheat the grill, preferably with hardwood or hardwood charcoal.

Crack open the salt crust with a hammer or the back of a knife, and peel it away. Transfer the pork belly to a cutting board, and cut into 1-inch-thick slices. Grill the pork belly slices, turning occasionally, until grill marks appear, about 12 minutes total. Serve the pork belly with the romesco sauce.

PORK BELLY AL ASADOR
with Salsa Verde

When you have access to high-quality pork, there is very little you need to do to let it shine. After an overnight brine, the meat gets grilled over hardwood, picking up plenty of smoke, before it is seared and served with a bright and herby Salsa Verde (page 116).

SERVES 10 AS A SMALL PLATE

2 quarts Heavy Brine (page 249)
1 (3-pound) fresh pork belly
Salsa Verde (page 116)

Place the pork belly in the brine and refrigerate overnight.

Preheat the grill, preferably with hardwood or hardwood charcoal. Remove the pork belly from the brine and pat dry. Grill the pork belly, moving it between direct and indirect heat, until charred on the outside and cooked through, but not falling apart, about 2½ hours. Let the pork belly cool slightly.

Slice the pork belly ½-inch thick pieces. Heat a nonstick skillet over medium-high heat. Sear the slices of pork belly, turning once, until golden, about 8 minutes. Transfer the pork belly slices to a platter as seared, then top with the Salsa Verde and serve.

MORTEAU SAUSAGE

This classic French sausage is cured by fermentation then gently smoked. The level of salt used—1.7% of the weight of the meats—keeps any dangerous bacteria at bay. Traditionally, Morteau sausage is smoked over juniper wood, but we use the hardwoods available at Wyebrook and add juniper to the meats. Serve this in Pork Pot au Feu (page 26) or as part of a charcuterie plate.

MAKES ABOUT 4 POUNDS

3¼ pounds pork shoulder, cut into cubes

12 ounces pork fatback, cut into cubes

1½ ounces fresh pork skin, coarsely chopped

5 teaspoons fine sea salt (32 grams)

1½ tablespoons ground juniper berries

1 teaspoon finely ground black pepper

About 4 feet of beef casings

EQUIPMENT: **Meat grinder, sausage stuffer, hardwood smoker, hardwood chips such as cherry, apple, or oak**

Arrange the pork shoulder, fatback, and skin on a baking sheet and put in the freezer until the edges of the meat just start to freeze (the center should not be frozen), about 30 minutes.

Stir together the salt, juniper, and pepper in a bowl. Toss the meats with the spice mixture. Grind the meats together using a ⅛-inch die on a meat grinder and let fall into a chilled bowl set over ice.

Cut the casings into three 16-inch lengths. Make a knot on one end of each casing. Using a sausage stuffer, fill the casings with the filling. Using kitchen string, tie off the open ends of the casings, making a loop with the string so the sausages can hang. Hang the sausages at cool room temperature for 12 to 18 hours. Transfer the sausage to a sealed container and refrigerate for 2 days to ferment.

Preheat a hardwood smoker to 180°F.

Smoke the sausages, replenishing the smoker with hardwood chips as needed, for 8 to 12 hours. Chill the sausages until ready to serve.

BACON-WRAPPED PORK LIVER
with Chile Sauce

Pork liver's silky texture and mild flavor make it a delicacy in many cultures. We like to serve it with a vinegar-chile syrup, reminiscent of Pennsylvania Dutch–style hot pepper sauces, and grilled wedges of acorn squash, which are in season when we hold La Tuade. A few minutes over a hardwood fire plumps the meat and graces it with a wisp of smoke, resulting in a sweetly spicy bite of pig.

SERVES 12 TO 16 AS AN APPETIZER OR SMALL PLATE

15 dried hot red chiles, such as Thai, cayenne, or chile de arbol, or 2 tablespoons dried red chile flakes

2 cups sugar

2 cups apple cider vinegar

Fine sea salt and freshly ground black pepper

1 acorn squash, halved and seeded

1¼ pounds pork liver

16 bacon slices

To make the chile sauce, pulse the dried chiles in a spice grinder until coarsely ground, then place them in a heavy saucepan. Stir in the sugar, vinegar, and ½ teaspoon salt, then bring to a boil. Boil the sauce until it has reduced to a syrupy consistency and measures about 2 cups, 10 to 15 minutes. Remove from the heat and let cool.

Preheat the grill, preferably with hardwood or hardwood charcoal. Grill the squash, moving it between direct and indirect heat, until charred in places and tender, 35 to 45 minutes. Let the squash cool slightly, then cut into 1-inch-thick wedges. Add wood or charcoal to the fire if necessary.

Cut the liver into 16 (2-inch) pieces, then wrap each piece in a slice of bacon. Thread each piece of bacon-wrapped liver onto a wooden skewer, then season generously with salt and pepper. Grill the skewers over indirect heat until the liver is just cooked through and has a creamy texture, 6 to 8 minutes. Remove from the grill and let stand for 5 minutes.

Drizzle some of the chile sauce over each skewer and serve with a wedge of squash.

PORK POT AU FEU

Pot au feu, a simple dish of beef and vegetables, is a classic at every French table. We've mixed things up by using pork, including our fermented and smoked Morteau Sausage (page 24), and by charring the seasonal vegetables separately in a hardwood fire. The meats and vegetables are gently reheated in pork stock, which becomes an extra flavorful first course. Serve the stock in bowls, sprinkled with a little nutmeg, before diving into the meats and vegetables.

SERVES 12

FOR THE VEGETABLES

1 pound large onions, unpeeled

2 large celery roots

1 pound sweet potatoes

1 pound purple-top turnips

1 pound carrots

1 small Napa cabbage, quartered

FOR THE MEATS AND BROTH

3 quarts Rich Pork Stock (page 245)

1 Morteau Sausage (page 24), cut into ½-inch-thick slices

1 Smoked Pork Loin (page 32), cut into ½-inch-thick slices

Horseradish Mustard Cream (page 215), for serving

Grill the vegetables: Preheat a grill, preferably with hardwood or hardwood charcoal. Let the fire burn down to embers. Spread the embers and ash evenly across the bottom of the grill, then add more hardwood or charcoal to one side of the grill, letting it continue to burn. Place all the vegetables except the cabbage in the ashes next to the fire, arranging the onions closest to the flame, then the celery roots, followed by the sweet potatoes, turnips, and finally the carrots. Place the grate over the fire and place the cabbage on the grate, over the other vegetables. Grill the vegetables, spreading the embers and ash and adding hardwood to the fire as needed, until they are charred and tender. The cabbage will take about 25 minutes and will require turning. The other vegetables will take between 45 minutes and 1½ hours. Check and turn the vegetables occasionally. Transfer the vegetables to a large bowl as they are done. Rinse the vegetables with water to remove any ash, then peel and cut into 1-inch pieces.

Dean welcomes visitors to one of Wyebrook's guest chef dinners and talks about the ethos of the farm.

Prepare the meats and broth: Bring the stock to a simmer in a large pot and season to taste with salt. Place the vegetables in the stock and simmer gently until heated through, about 10 minutes. Use a slotted spoon to transfer the vegetables to a large serving platter and cover loosely to keep warm. Bring the stock back to a gentle simmer, then add the sausage and pork loin and simmer until heated through, about 5 minutes. Transfer the meats to the platter. Ladle some of the stock over the vegetables and the meats and serve with horseradish-mustard cream on the side.

LA TUADE: Pig Killing Day

In the morning, the fog is heavy and flows down the pastures and into the valley that cradles the brook. The farm is still and closing itself down for the coming winter. There is the waft of woodsmoke from a fire, which is warming a cauldron filled with water—the means by which we remove the pig's hair after it is killed.

Pig killing day—*la tuade*—is a day of celebration and community, a Thanksgiving of sorts. Though it does not happen so much in this country any more, you can still find these autumnal gatherings in the French countryside. There is a beautiful book, *Pork & Sons*, by a Frenchman named Stéphane Reynaud that chronicles the pig killing. His story and tradition, passed down through generations, was the original inspiration for Wyebrook's La Tuade.

Over 100,000,000 pigs were slaughtered for food in 2014. But almost none of them were killed on a farm, in front of 30 people longing for a deeper, more tangible connection with their food. The day begins with the words of Wendell Berry, "Let them stand still for the bullet, and stare the shooter in the eye…" and ends with a suitably poetic meal. What happens in between far exceeds what words can capture, requiring presence of both body and mind. It is visual, visceral, emotional—something closer to how we would like to think our ancestors connected with the source of their food. Today, life is less about day-to-day survival, but no less about respect for the farmer, butcher, cook, and most importantly, the animal. And this is what we celebrate.

The small crowd gathers around a pig that has been stunned and is now lifeless, watching its blood pool into a metal bowl. Later, that will become a course of blood sausage. These same people will help lower the pig into the cauldron, then scrape away its hair. They will watch as it's eviscerated, knowing that its organs—heart and liver, lungs and kidneys—will compose some of what they will dine on later. As the hog is split into two even sides, revealing its more recognizable parts, loin and belly, shoulder and ham, La Tuade reveals its most glorious moment—the transformation of pig into pork. And through it all, we are together. We are strangers in the morning and family by the night. *—Bryan*

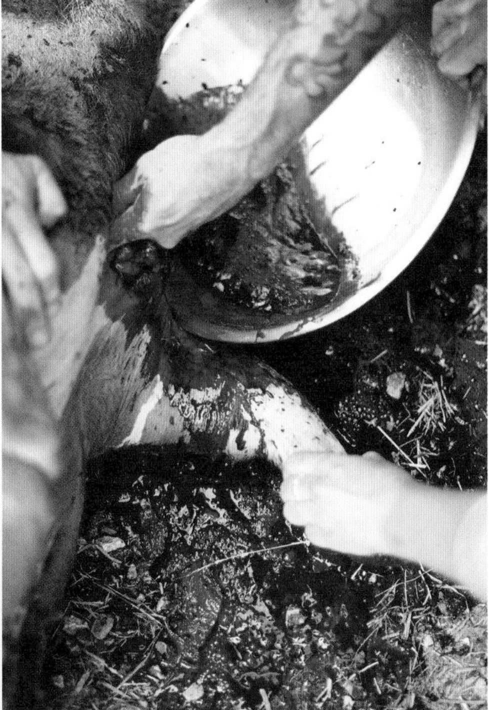

BLOOD SAUSAGE

Once a year, at La Tuade, we are lucky enough to be able to cook with blood (the rest of the time, our animals are slaughtered at USDA-inspected facilities, and we don't have access to their blood). This classic dish feels right at home here in Pennsylvania thanks to the addition of spiceberries, a native plant whose fruit tastes of pepper and allspice. Serve this delicate sausage with Pickled Bull's Blood Beets and Onions (page 173) for a fun play on words and flavors. Look for pig's blood at your local butcher shop, or Asian markets.

SERVES 8 TO 12

1 quart pig's blood, blended if coagulated

1¼ cups heavy cream

1 onion, chopped

1 cup fresh or dried breadcrumbs

½ cup almond flour

2 tablespoons walnut pieces, preferably black walnuts

2 tablespoons cocoa powder

1 teaspoon fresh thyme leaves

½ teaspoon ground cinnamon

4 spiceberries, ground (or a combination of 2 allspice berries and 2 black peppercorns)

A pinch of red chile flakes

Fine sea salt

1½ cups diced pork fatback

Preheat the oven to 350°F. Place a large baking pan in the oven and fill it halfway with hot water. Line a 9 x 5-inch loaf pan with plastic wrap, leaving a few inches of overhang.

Combine the blood, cream, onions, breadcrumbs, almond flour, walnuts, cocoa powder, thyme, cinnamon, spiceberries, chile flakes, and 1½ teaspoons salt in a blender and purée until smooth. Transfer the blood mixture to a bowl and stir in the fatback. Pour the blood mixture into the prepared pan, then fold the overhanging plastic over it. Cover the loaf pan with aluminum foil. Place the loaf pan in the water bath in the oven and bake until the blood sausage is set, 1½ to 1¾ hours. Remove the loaf pan from the water bath and let cool completely at room temperature, about 1 hour.

To serve, unmold the blood sausage, discarding the plastic wrap. Slice the sausage and transfer to a serving platter. Serve at room temperature.

SMOKED PORK LOIN

The loin is one of the leanest parts of the pig, which means it can dry out easily. We brine it overnight for extra moisture and flavor, then smoke it over hardwood chips, which adds a subtle layer of smolder. Serve this as part of Pork Pot au Feu (page 26) or by itself with a side of Horseradish Mustard Cream (page 215). Leftovers are perfect for sandwiches.

SERVES 6 TO 8

1 (2½-pound) boneless pork loin

8 cups Heavy Brine (page 249)

EQUIPMENT: **Hardwood smoker, hardwood chips such as cherry, apple, or oak**

Place the pork loin in the brine and refrigerate overnight.

Preheat the smoker to 180°F. Remove the pork from the brine, then pat dry. Smoke the loin, replenishing the smoker with hardwood chips as needed, for 1 hour.

To serve, cut the pork loin into thin slices.

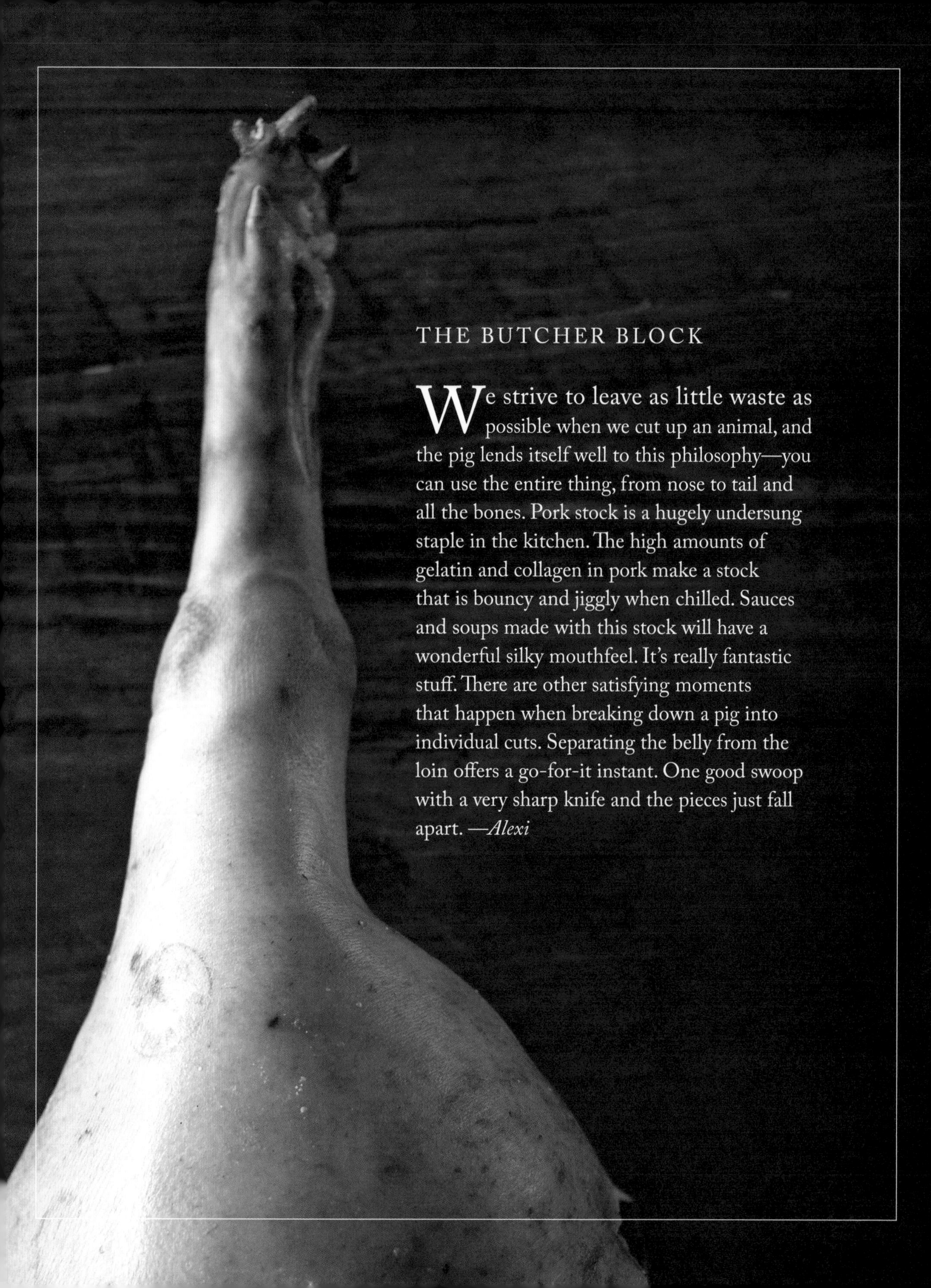

THE BUTCHER BLOCK

We strive to leave as little waste as possible when we cut up an animal, and the pig lends itself well to this philosophy—you can use the entire thing, from nose to tail and all the bones. Pork stock is a hugely undersung staple in the kitchen. The high amounts of gelatin and collagen in pork make a stock that is bouncy and jiggly when chilled. Sauces and soups made with this stock will have a wonderful silky mouthfeel. It's really fantastic stuff. There are other satisfying moments that happen when breaking down a pig into individual cuts. Separating the belly from the loin offers a go-for-it instant. One good swoop with a very sharp knife and the pieces just fall apart. —*Alexi*

A few of Wyebrook's pigs forage under the shady trees that edge the farm's pastures; some of the pork will be sold fresh and some will be cured for later use.

GNOCCHI ROTELLA
with Black Olive Relish

Gnocchi dough encases a rich ragu of organs and fresh ricotta for a most intriguing take on meat and potatoes. The briny relish balances and rounds out each bite. Unless you're slaughtering your own pig, you'll have difficulty finding lung. No worries—this recipe is equally delicious without it.

SERVES 10 TO 12

FOR THE FILLING

1 pork heart, halved

2 pork kidneys

1 pork lung, if available

Fine sea salt and freshly ground black pepper

8 cups Rich Pork Stock (page 245) or Rich Chicken Stock (page 246); if not using a lung, use only 4 cups stock

3 garlic cloves, chopped

2 tablespoons unsalted butter or extra-virgin olive oil

1 onion, chopped

2 cups Fresh Ricotta Cheese (page 240)

2 tablespoons finely chopped flat-leaf parsley

1 teaspoon finely chopped fresh thyme leaves

FOR THE GNOCCHI DOUGH

2 pounds Yukon Gold potatoes

¼ cup coarse sea salt

2 large eggs, lightly beaten

1½ cups all-purpose flour

1 cup finely grated Parmigiano Reggiano

½ cup (1 stick) unsalted butter, melted and cooled

Fine sea salt

¼ cup rendered animal fat or extra-virgin olive oil

FOR THE BLACK OLIVE RELISH

½ cup pitted Kalamata olives

⅓ cup cornichons

3 tablespoons capers in brine, drained

3 tablespoons extra-virgin olive oil

2 teaspoons whole-grain mustard

2 teaspoons finely grated orange zest

EQUIPMENT: **Meat grinder**

Make the filling: Preheat a grill, preferably with hardwood or hardwood charcoal. Season the heart, kidneys, and lung (if using) with ¼ teaspoon each salt and pepper, then grill over direct heat, turning once, until charred on the outside, 10 to 12 minutes.

Bring the stock to a simmer in a medium saucepan, then add the heart, kidneys, and lung, and simmer until cooked through, 12 to 15 minutes. Remove the organs from the stock and let cool slightly. Grind the organs with the garlic using a ⅛-inch die on a meat grinder. (Alternatively, you can very finely chop the meats and garlic together.) Place the ground mixture in a large bowl.

Heat the butter in a large heavy skillet over medium heat, then add the onions and ½ teaspoon each salt and pepper, and cook, stirring occasionally, until translucent, about 5 minutes. Add the onions to the ground meats in the bowl. Stir in the ricotta, parsley, and thyme and season with salt and pepper to taste.

Make the gnocchi dough: Preheat the oven to 425°F. Place the potatoes on a baking sheet, then sprinkle with the coarse sea salt. Roast the potatoes until tender, about 1 hour. Let cool slightly, then peel. Force the potatoes through a ricer into a bowl, then stir in the eggs, flour, cheese, butter, and ½ teaspoon salt to form a dough.

Place a large sheet of aluminum foil on a work surface, then place overlapping sheets of plastic wrap over the foil. Transfer the gnocchi dough to the plastic wrap and pat with floured hands into a rough rectangle. Lightly flour the surface of the dough, and using a floured rolling pin, roll the dough into a 15 x 12-inch rectangle. Spread the ragu evenly over the dough, leaving a 1-inch border on the long sides of the rectangle. Using the plastic and foil as a guide, roll the dough up and around the filling, like a jellyroll. Shape the dough into a thick cylinder wrapped in the plastic and foil, squeezing and tightening the ends of the foil to enclose the gnocchi.

Bring a large pot or a fish-poacher of water to a simmer. Place the gnocchi cylinder in the simmering water and poach, turning frequently so it will cook evenly, for 35 minutes. Let the gnocchi cool slightly, then unwrap and cut into 1-inch-thick slices.

Heat the rendered fat in a large heavy nonstick skillet over medium-high heat until hot. Working in batches, sear the gnocchi slices, turning once, until golden brown, about 6 minutes total. Transfer to a serving platter.

While the gnocchi poaches, make the relish: Combine the olives, cornichons, capers, oil, mustard, and orange zest in a food processor and pulse until coarsely chopped.

Serve the gnocchi slices topped with the relish.

PIG'S HEAD TORCHON

If you're looking for a culinary adventure, start here. Pigs' heads are packed with flavor and intriguing texture, and using them speaks to our waste-nothing ethos of whole animal cooking. This recipe requires some hands-on work that is not typical in most home kitchens, but the results are truly delicious. The torchon—the word means "dish towel" in French and refers to the wrapping in fabric to create a cylindrical shape—contains all the edible parts of the head (save the remaining bones to make stock). Pig's heads are easy to get—ask your butcher to halve it for access to all the meats. We like to serve slices of torchon as a main course, paired with Green Coriander-Lima Bean Ragout (page 42), Salt-Baked Yukon Golds (page 44), and Pig's Ear Tomato Salsa (page 44).

EACH TORCHON SERVES 12

1 fresh pig's head, halved lengthwise (ask your butcher to do this for you)

4 cups Heavy Brine (page 249)

2 to 3 quarts Rich Pork Stock (page 245) or Rich Chicken Stock (page 246)

EQUIPMENT: **Meat slicer**

Remove the ears from the pig's head and reserve for another use (such as Pig's Ear Tomato Salsa, page 44). Make an incision down the length of the front of the head, if necessary (this may have been done for you if your butcher has halved the head). Carefully remove the skin in two whole pieces with a sharp knife (the left side and the right side). Bone the pig's head, removing the cheeks, tongue, and brain. Reserve the bones for stock. Using the tip of a sharp knife, score the flesh side of the pork skin then place the skin, meats, and brain in a large resealable plastic bag. Add the brine and seal. Refrigerate, turning the bag every day, for 5 days.

Discard the brine, then pat the skin, meats, and brain dry. Cut the tongue in half lengthwise, and halve the brain.

Lay a large piece of cheesecloth on a work surface. Lay one piece of the pork skin on the cheesecloth. Fold the skin as needed to create a large rectangle. Place 1 cheek, half of the tongue, and half of the brain along the center of the skin, then tightly roll the skin around the meats and brain to form a cylinder. Wrap the cheesecloth tightly around the torchon then secure the ends of the cylinder with kitchen string. Tie the cylinder at 2-inch intervals with string. Repeat with the remaining piece of skin, meats, and brain. Hang the torchons at cool room temperature to ferment overnight.

Heat the stock in a large heavy pot to 180°F (use a candy or deep-fry thermometer to regulate the water temperature), then place the torchons in the hot stock and poach for 4 hours. Cool the torchons, then chill completely.

To serve, slice the torchons very thinly using a meat slicer or a very sharp knife. Serve cold.

LIMA BEAN RAGOUT WITH GREEN CORIANDER

This braised lima bean dish cleverly uses fresh pork skin and whey (left over from making ricotta cheese, page 240) to produce an extraordinarily silky sauce. If you don't have access to green coriander seeds, regular ones will work fine.

SERVES 6 TO 8

2 tablespoons extra-virgin olive oil

1 medium onion, diced

1 pound fresh or frozen lima beans (about 3 cups)

8 ounces fresh pork skin, quartered

2 cups whey (page 240)

1 cup Rich Pork Stock (page 245)

2 tablespoons Dried Green Coriander (page 238), crushed

Fine sea salt and freshly ground black pepper

Heat the oil in a large heavy skillet over medium heat until hot. Add the onion and cook, stirring occasionally, until translucent, about 5 minutes. Add the lima beans, pork skin, whey, stock, coriander, and ¼ teaspoon each salt and pepper. Bring to a simmer and cook until the lima beans and pork skin are tender, about 45 minutes. Purée the skin and about a quarter of the lima bean liquid in a blender until very smooth, then pour back into the lima bean mixture. Season to taste with salt.

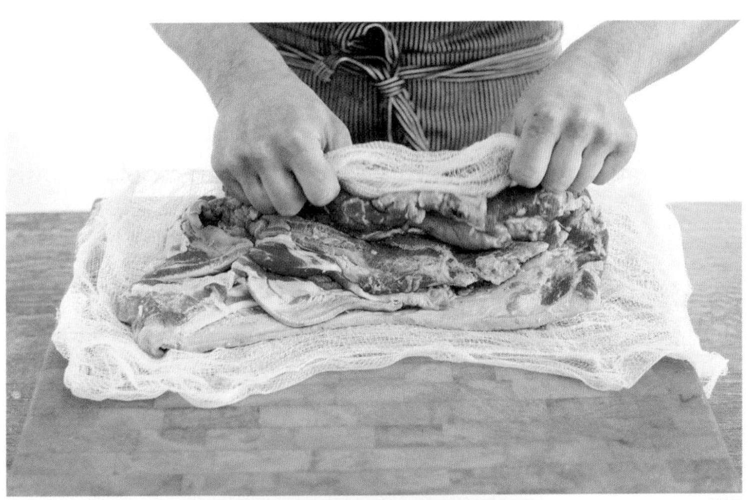

SALT-BAKED YUKON GOLDS

Baking potatoes in a mound of salt allows just enough seasoning to penetrate the skins, resulting in a intensely flavorful, surprisingly simple side dish.

SERVES 12

5 pounds Yukon Gold potatoes

About 4 pounds kosher salt

Sour cream or unsalted butter, for serving

Preheat the oven to 400°F.

Spread a ½-inch layer of kosher salt in a deep roasting pan. Nestle the potatoes in the salt and cover with the remaining salt. Bake in the center of the oven until tender, about 1¼ hours.

Carefully brush off the salt, then peel and slice the potatoes. Transfer the potatoes to a platter. Serve with sour cream or unsalted butter.

PIG'S EAR TOMATO SALSA

This unctuous sauce goes beautifully with our Pici Pasta (page 211).

MAKES ABOUT 1 QUART

2 fresh pig's ears

2 cups rendered pork fat, melted

4 cups Roasted Tomato Purée (page 230)

2 large garlic cloves, thickly sliced

Fine sea salt and freshly ground black pepper

Place the pig's ears in the rendered fat in a medium saucepan and bring to a simmer. Gently cook the pig's ears in the fat until very tender, about 4 hours. Remove from the heat and cool slightly. Slice the pig's ears into ¼-inch-thick strips. Reserve the fat.

Bring the tomato purée and garlic to a simmer in a large heavy skillet. Add the sliced pig's ears and the reserved fat. Simmer the sauce until thickened and emulsified, about 1 hour. Season to taste with salt and pepper.

TUSCAN-STYLE SAUSAGE

Fresh pork skin adds a welcome chew to this hot Italian classic. This sausage is equally suitable as the base for a quick pasta sauce as it is simply grilled with onions and peppers.

MAKES ABOUT 3 POUNDS

2 pounds boneless pork shoulder, cut into cubes

12 ounces pork fatback, cut into cubes

8 ounces fresh pork skin, coarsely chopped

2 tablespoons fennel seeds

1 tablespoon dried red chile flakes

Fine sea salt and freshly ground black pepper

About 5 feet of hog casings

3 tablespoons rendered animal fat or vegetable oil

EQUIPMENT: **Meat grinder, sausage stuffer, a pin**

Place the pork shoulder, fatback, and skin on a baking sheet and put in the freezer until the edges of the meat just start to freeze (the center should not be frozen), about 30 minutes.

Stir together the fennel seeds, chile flakes, 1 tablespoon salt, and ½ teaspoon pepper in a bowl. Toss the meats with the spice mixture, then grind the meats together using a ⅛-inch die on a meat grinder, letting the meats fall into a chilled bowl set over ice.

Using a sausage stuffer, fill the casings with the filling, twisting the casings to make 8-inch links. Prick each link 2 or 3 times with the pin. Chill until ready to cook.

To cook, preheat a large griddle over medium-high heat. Brush the griddle with some of the rendered fat, then cook the sausages, turning occasionally, until golden browned and cooked through, 8 to 10 minutes.

Toulouse
Morteau
Chicken Boudin Blanc

Tuscan
Blood
Merguez

SAUSAGES 101

There are seemingly infinite variations on the theme of sausage, but with few exceptions (like blood sausage), there are basic guidelines that can help simplify things to make it feel like less of a, well . . . a grind.

THE EQUIPMENT

A meat grinder, preferably with varying holed dies: ⅛-inch and ¼-inch dies are the most useful

A sausage stuffer

A sharp pin (used to prick the sausages)

THE INGREDIENTS

Meat (typically 75% to 80% of the mixture)

Fat (typically 20% to 25% of the mixture)

Seasonings (salt, spices, wine, herbs)

Filler (breadcrumbs, cheese)

Casings (hog or beef)

If you've never made your own sausage from scratch, the process might seem intimidating, but each step is in fact quite simple and straightforward. The first step is to decide what style of sausage you're going for. Merguez (page 117), a heavily spiced lamb sausage, has no filler, which makes it taste very meaty, whereas the Toulouse sausage (page 52) is flavored with only garlic and little wine and has breadcrumbs for a finer mouthfeel. There are very finely ground sausages like Chicken Boudin Blanc (page 148) that require a food processor instead of a meat grinder, but here we'll focus on the coarser style grinds of sausage.

Once you've decided on the direction you're headed, follow the steps below:

Cut and chill: Cut the meat and fat into 1-inch pieces, big enough to fit into the meat grinder. Spread the meat and fat on baking sheets and place them in the freezer for about 30 minutes—until the edges of the meat just start to freeze, but the centers remain unfrozen. This prevents the fat from melting and smearing due to heat caused by friction in the grinder.

Season: Toss the meat and fat together with the seasonings so that they will be evenly distributed as the meat and fat are ground.

Grind: Put the meat and fat through a meat grinder fit with the appropriate sized die. Place a chilled bowl set inside a bowl of ice under the grinder to catch the meat and prevent it from becoming too warm, which again, might melt the fat. Chill the sausage filling.

At this point, it's a good idea to fry up a little of the mixture to make sure the seasonings are correct. Take 1 tablespoon of the sausage mixture and cook it in a small skillet until cooked through. Taste the sausage and adjust the mixture's seasonings accordingly.

Fill: Feed the casings onto the nozzle of a sausage stuffer by finding one end of the casing and looping it over the nozzle, then feeding the rest of the casing onto the nozzle. This process goes more smoothly if the nozzle is wet. Once the casing is fed all the way onto the nozzle, pull about 2 inches back toward you and make a knot in the casing. Feed the casing back onto the nozzle until the knot stops you from going any further. Make a hole with a pin in the end of the casing to let any air out. Stuff the filling into the casings with the sausage stuffer, twisting the sausage alternating forwards and backwards (towards you and away from you) to make links. Prick each link 2 to 3 times with the pin to prevent the sausages from exploding when cooked. Chill the sausage until you're ready to cook.

SPAGHETTI
with Tuscan-Style Sausage and Mushrooms

This rich sauce only takes a few minutes to throw together—that is, after you make the sausage. If you just want to get dinner on the table, substitute any spicy Italian-style sausage meat. But please consider making the pasta from scratch—its richness and chew is unparalleled. If you can get your hands on a chitarra (guitar) pasta cutter, now is the time to use it. If not, a regular spaghetti cutter will do the trick.

SERVES 6

12 ounces fresh Spaghetti (page 206)

1 pound Tuscan-Style Sausage, casings removed (page 45)

8 ounces wild mushrooms, trimmed and torn into small pieces

1 cup heavy cream

Fine sea salt and freshly ground black pepper

3 tablespoons flat-leaf parsley leaves

½ cup finely grated Parmigiano Reggiano

Cook the spaghetti in boiling salted water until al dente. Reserve 1½ cups pasta cooking water, then drain the pasta.

Heat a dry large heavy skillet over medium-high heat until hot. Add the sausage in an even layer and cook, undisturbed, until well browned on the bottom, 4 to 6 minutes. Stir in the mushrooms, breaking up the sausage, and cook until the mushrooms give off any moisture and begin to brown, about 5 minutes. Add about 1 cup of the pasta cooking water, scraping up any browned bits from the bottom of the pan. Stir in the cream and simmer until slightly thickened, about 2 minutes. Season the sauce with salt and pepper to taste. Stir in the cooked pasta and parsley, tossing to coat. Serve the pasta topped with the Parmigiano Reggiano.

TOULOUSE SAUSAGE AND FRENCH FRY SANDWICHES

This sandwich might taste like a ballpark classic, but Andrew actually discovered it on an eating expedition in Provence, where he came upon a local vendor selling foot-long pork and garlic sausages on a roll topped with a heavy hand of fries. We like to add a smear of mayonnaise and Dijon-Style Mustard (page 214) to the crusty rolls. Smoking the sausage adds an extra layer of flavor, but you can omit this step if you like.

MAKES ABOUT 3½ POUNDS SAUSAGE OR 6 (FOOT-LONG) SANDWICHES

FOR THE SAUSAGE

2 pounds boneless pork shoulder, cut into cubes

12 ounces pork fatback, cut into cubes

8 ounces bacon, chopped

1 cup fresh breadcrumbs

4 cloves garlic, finely chopped

¼ cup cold red wine

1 teaspoon finely chopped fresh thyme

1 teaspoon sugar

½ teaspoon ground mace

Fine sea salt and freshly ground black pepper

About 6½ feet of hog casings

FOR THE SANDWICHES

3 tablespoons rendered animal fat or vegetable oil

6 (12-inch) crusty rolls

Mayonnaise

Dijon-Style Mustard (page 214)

Freshly fried French fries

EQUIPMENT: **Meat grinder, sausage stuffer, a pin, hardwood smoker (optional), hardwood chips such as cherry, apple, or oak (optional)**

Arrange the pork shoulder, fatback, and bacon on a baking sheet and put in the freezer until the edges of the meat just start to freeze (the center should still be frozen), about 30 minutes.

Stones cleared from the surrounding fields make up the sturdy walls of Wyebrook's early Pennsylvania farmhouse, barn, and outbuildings.

Stir together the breadcrumbs, garlic, red wine, thyme, sugar, mace, 1 teaspoon salt and ¾ teaspoon pepper in a bowl.

Grind the pork, fatback, and bacon together using a ⅛-inch die on a meat grinder letting the meats fall into a chilled bowl set over ice. Stir in the breadcrumb mixture by hand until it is well combined.

Using a sausage stuffer, fill the casings with the filling, twisting the casings to make 12-inch links. Prick each link 2 or 3 times with the pin.

If smoked sausage is desired, preheat a hardwood smoker to 160°F.

Smoke the sausages, replenishing the smoker with hardwood chips as needed, for 8 to 12 hours. Chill the sausages until ready to serve.

To make the sandwiches, preheat a large griddle over medium-high heat. Brush the griddle with some of the rendered fat, then cook the sausages, turning occasionally, until golden browned and cooked through, 8 to 10 minutes.

Spread mayonnaise and mustard on the rolls, add the sausages and top with plenty of French fries.

RIGATONI

with Pork Liver and Ramp Ragu

Meat sauce usually takes hours to build depth, but substituting pork liver for ground meat adds richness in minutes. We enliven the sauce with ramps, a wild leek prized by foragers and cooks for its gentle onion perfume, during the late spring months when they are in season. A last-minute squeeze of lemon adds brightness.

SERVES 4 TO 6

1 pound fresh pork liver

4 ounces smoked pancetta or bacon, chopped

1 bunch ramps or scallions, bulbs sliced and greens coarsely chopped

2 tablespoons extra-virgin olive oil

A pinch of dried red chile flakes

1½ cups Roasted Tomato Purée (page 230)

1 tablespoon unsalted butter

Fine sea salt and freshly ground black pepper

12 ounces rigatoni

½ a lemon

EQUIPMENT: **Meat grinder**

Grind the liver and pancetta together using a ¼-inch die on a meat grinder, letting the meats fall into a bowl.

Heat a dry large heavy skillet over high heat until hot, then add the liver and pancetta and cook, undisturbed, until browned on the bottom, 2 to 3 minutes. Add the ramp bulbs, oil, and chile flakes and cook, scraping any browned bits from the bottom of the pan, 1 minute. Stir in the tomato purée and simmer until slightly thickened, about 2 minutes, then stir in the butter. Season the sauce with salt and pepper to taste. Keep warm over low heat.

Cook the rigatoni in boiling salted water until al dente. Reserve 1½ cups pasta cooking water, then drain the pasta. Stir the pasta into the sauce and toss to coat, adding some of the reserved pasta cooking water if needed. Squeeze the lemon over the pasta and serve.

PORK BELLY AND WINTER SQUASH SOUP

A few basic ingredients arrange themselves into a perfect picture of peasant-style comfort food. We use whey as the liquid base of the soup, but you can use chicken broth or even water. Leaving the pork belly and squash in chunks makes for a rustic bowl of soup; for a more refined version, blitz everything together in the blender until very smooth.

SERVES 6 TO 8

1½ pounds fresh pork belly, skin removed

Fine sea salt and freshly ground black pepper

1½ pounds onions, chopped

⅓ cup grade B maple syrup

2½ pounds winter squash, such as butternut or kabocha, peeled, seeded and cut into 1½-inch chunks

8 cups whey (page 240)

1 tablespoon crushed dried sage leaves

Cut the pork belly into ½-inch pieces, then put into a dry heavy pot and toss with 1 teaspoon salt. Cook the pork belly over medium heat, stirring occasionally, until golden brown, 8 to 10 minutes. Using a slotted spoon, transfer the pork belly to a platter and set aside. Pour off all but 2 tablespoons of fat from the pot (reserve the fat for another use).

Add the onions to the remaining fat in the pot, stirring and scraping up any browned bits, and cook, stirring occasionally, until golden brown, about 6 minutes. Stir in the maple syrup and bring to a boil. Boil the syrup until it is several shades darker and thicker, about 6 minutes. Add the squash, whey, sage, and reserved pork belly, then bring to a simmer and cook until the squash is very tender, about 45 minutes. Season the soup with salt and pepper to taste, then serve.

CONFIT GARLIC SFORMATO

with Shaved Salami and Arugula

The simplest farm ingredients—butter, milk, eggs, and garlic—are transformed into light-as-air, savory flans. We serve this version, year-round, for lunch and brunch, but it would also make a fantastic cheese course.

SERVES 12

3 tablespoons unsalted butter

2 tablespoons plus 1 teaspoon all-purpose flour

3 cups whole milk

4 large eggs, lightly beaten

¾ cup finely grated Parmigiano Reggiano

4 cloves Garlic Confit (page 243), mashed to a paste

Fine sea salt

4 cups arugula

2 tablespoons extra-virgin olive oil

1 tablespoon fresh lemon juice

1 cup shaved salami

Preheat the oven to 325°F. Butter 12 (½-cup) muffin cups or a 9 x 5-inch loaf pan.

Heat the butter in a heavy saucepan over medium heat until melted. Whisk in the flour and cook, whisking frequently, until the flour is pale golden and fragrant, about 6 minutes. Add the milk in a slow stream, whisking constantly, and bring to a boil. Reduce the heat to a simmer and cook, stirring frequently, until thickened, about 10 minutes. Remove the saucepan from the heat and let the béchamel cool slightly. Whisk in the eggs, cheese, mashed garlic confit, and ¾ teaspoon salt.

Place a large roasting pan in the oven and fill it halfway with hot water. Pour the batter into the muffin cups, then place the muffin pan in the roasting pan. Bake until the flans are set but still wobbly in the center, about 30 minutes for muffin cups and 1 hour for a loaf pan. Transfer to a rack to cool slightly. (Flans can be made ahead and reheated in a 250°F oven until warmed through.)

Run a knife around the edges of the pan, then gently turn out the flans (if baked in a loaf pan, cut into slices). Toss the arugula with the oil, lemon juice, and ¼ teaspoon salt. Serve the flans with the arugula salad and the shaved salami.

PANADE *with Grilled Onions and Mushrooms*

The inspiration for this savory bread pudding comes from a classic Richard Olney recipe, published in his book, *Simple French Food*. Serve this comforting dish with a brightly dressed green salad.

SERVES 8 TO 10

2 red onions, halved crosswise

8 ounces oyster mushrooms, torn into hand-sized clusters

1 pound sourdough bread, cut into 1½-inch cubes

4 tablespoons unsalted butter, melted

4 cups Rich Pork Stock (page 245)

1½ cups finely grated Parmigiano Reggiano

1 cup grated Gruyère cheese

Preheat the grill, preferably with hardwood or hardwood charcoal. Let the fire burn down to embers. Spread the embers and ash evenly across the bottom of the grill, then add more hardwood or charcoal to one side of the grill, letting it continue to burn. Place the onions skin side down in the coals, with the cut side exposed, and cook until the skins are charred and the onions are tender, about 45 minutes. Remove from the grill.

Place the mushrooms on the grill over direct heat and grill until the clusters are charred on the outside and tender inside, 10 to 12 minutes. Remove from the grill and season with salt and pepper to taste.

Preheat the oven to 350°F. Butter a large baking dish.

Spread the bread in one layer on a large baking sheet, then toast in the oven until golden, about 10 minutes. Transfer the bread to a large bowl and toss with the melted butter.

Peel and coarsely chop the onions, then toss with the bread. Tear the mushrooms into bite-sized pieces, then stir into the bread mixture. Spread the bread mixture evenly in the baking dish, then pour the pork stock over the bread and sprinkle with the cheeses. Bake the panade until the top is golden and the bread has absorbed all the stock, about 1 hour. Let the panade stand for 15 minutes to set. Cut into squares and serve.

ROSEMARY APPLE HAND TARTS

A pie crust made with lard has a tender flake and loads of flavor. A mix of apples ensures a well-balanced filling—we especially like Mutsu and Honeycrisp in this herb-enhanced filling, adapted from a recipe by Wyebrook Farm's former baker Nicole Viola.

SERVES 6

FOR THE CRUST

1¼ cups all-purpose flour

Fine sea salt

⅓ cup cold rendered pork fat

4 to 5 tablespoons cold water

FOR THE FILLING

1½ pounds apples, peeled, cored and thinly sliced

Juice of 1 lemon

⅓ cup granulated sugar

2 tablespoons all-purpose flour

½ teaspoon finely chopped fresh rosemary

½ teaspoon ground cinnamon

¼ teaspoon ground cloves

¼ teaspoon freshly grated nutmeg

3 dashes Angostura bitters

Fine sea salt

1 large egg, lightly beaten

Demerara sugar, for sprinkling

Make the crust: Whisk together the flour and ¼ teaspoon salt in a bowl. Work the cold lard into the flour with a rubber spatula, smearing and combining the lard and flour until the fat is mostly combined but still has some small, pea-sized lumps. (Alternatively, use a food processor to pulse together the ingredients.) Stir in 4 tablespoons water with a fork, then squeeze a small handful of the dough; if it is crumbly, stir in the remaining 1 tablespoon water.

(recipe continues)

Turn the dough out onto a work surface. Smear the dough with the palm of your hand across the work surface 3 or 4 times so that it comes together. Pat the dough into a round, then wrap it in plastic wrap and chill for at least 1 hour.

Make the filling: Combine the apples, lemon juice, granulated sugar, flour, rosemary, cinnamon, cloves, nutmeg, bitters, and ½ teaspoon salt in a medium saucepan. Cook over medium-low heat, stirring occasionally, until apples are slightly softened and mixture has thickened, about 10 minutes. Remove from the heat and let cool.

Preheat the oven to 350°F. Line a baking sheet with parchment paper.

Roll the dough out on a floured work surface with a floured rolling pin into large round. Using a small plate or cookie cutter, cut out six 5-inch rounds. Transfer the rounds to the lined baking sheet. Divide the filling evenly between the rounds, mounding it in the center of each piece of dough. Fold the edge of the dough over the filling, overlapping it as needed. Brush the edge of the dough with some of the egg wash then sprinkle with the demerara sugar. Repeat with the remaining tarts. Chill the filled tarts for at least 30 minutes to firm up.

Bake the tarts until the crust is golden brown and the filling is bubbling, 25 to 35 minutes. Let the tarts cool completely on a rack before serving.

YEAST-RAISED DOUGHNUTS

with Chocolate-Orange Dipping Sauce

This baby bottom–soft dough, based on Italian bombolini, substitutes lard for the more traditional butter. It's a dream to work with. A handful of candied oranges freshens up the chocolate dipping sauce, but a good-quality orange marmalade works well, too.

SERVES 6 TO 8

1 teaspoon active dry yeast

Scant ½ cup warm whole milk (105-115°F)

1½ cups all-purpose flour, plus additional for dusting

1 large egg

About 4 cups rendered pork fat

2 tablespoons sugar

Fine sea salt

1 cup heavy cream

8 ounces bittersweet chocolate, chopped

¼ cup chopped Candied Valencia Oranges with some of their syrup (page 237)

Confectioners' sugar, for dusting

EQUIPMENT: **A deep-fat thermometer**

Stir together the yeast and warm milk in a mixer bowl and let stand until foamy, about 5 minutes. Mix in ¾ cup of the flour at low speed until combined. Cover the bowl with a kitchen towel and let the dough rise in a draft-free place at warm room temperature until doubled in size and bubbles appear on the surface, about 1 hour.

Add the egg, 2 tablespoons of the pork fat, sugar, ½ teaspoon salt, and remaining ¾ cup flour and mix on low speed until combined. Increase the speed to medium and beat until smooth and elastic, 5 to 7 minutes. Scrape the dough into the center of the bowl and dust lightly with flour. Cover the bowl with the kitchen towel and let the dough rise at warm room temperature until doubled in size, about 1 hour.

Line a baking sheet with parchment or wax paper and lightly dust with flour. Punch down the dough and turn it out onto a lightly floured surface. Cut the dough into 16 equal pieces, form each into a ball, and place on the lined baking sheet.

Heat 2 inches of pork fat in a heavy saucepan over medium heat until it registers 350°F on a deep-fry thermometer. Fry the doughnuts in batches of 4, turning frequently, until puffed and golden, about 2 minutes per batch. Transfer the doughnuts with a slotted spoon to paper towels to drain. Return the oil to 350°F between batches.

Heat the cream and a pinch of salt in a small saucepan until it just comes to a boil. Place the chocolate in a bowl then pour the hot cream over the chocolate and let stand until melted, about 2 minutes. Whisk the chocolate and cream together until thoroughly combined, then stir in the chopped candied oranges. Dust the doughnuts with confectioners' sugar and serve with the chocolate-orange sauce.

BEEF

Pasture Perfect Flavor

In the last few decades as beef has been bred for the feedlot, the animals have gotten much bigger. Like most livestock, cattle are sold by weight—the bigger the animal, the more it is worth. These conventional breeds grow very quickly and require an enormous amount of calories. To that end, they are fed rations of high-energy corn and are administered growth hormones. Because of how they have been bred, these animals would have great difficulty thriving if they had to feed on pasture.

In contrast, Wyebrook cattle are raised completely on grass. We work towards making our pastures as nutritious as possible, but grass and clover have much less sugar than corn and so our animals gain weight more slowly than those raised in feedlots. When selecting animals to be raised on pasture, it is important to choose animals with the correct frame size. Because our animals can only ingest a limited amount of calories per day, due to a 100% grass-based system, we have to select those that have smaller frames, so they can finish (put on fat) as quickly as possible.

We love the Devon, an active, chestnut-colored breed with a smaller frame that excels at foraging. Because they put on fat faster than other breeds, Devons have recently fallen out of favor with commercial growers. But they work very well for us, especially when we cross them with more typical breeds like Angus. We end up with animals that finish well on grass, give us a higher yield, and have more hybrid vigor than purebreds. Even though these cattle finish relatively quickly for grass-fed animals, they still take longer than feedlot cattle. But the meat we produce is a higher quality and so much tastier, as is always the case with grass-fed breeds that are given proper time to mature. —*Dean*

BEEF CHEEK BORSCHT

Beef cheeks possess such a startling depth of flavor that we use water as the base for this borscht—as the cheeks braise, they create their own stock. Roasting the beets separately concentrates their flavor and keeps their sweet earthiness distinct.

SERVES 6 TO 8

2 pounds beef cheeks

Fine sea salt and freshly ground black pepper

2 tablespoons unsalted butter

3 celery ribs, chopped

2 onions, chopped

2 teaspoons caraway seeds

3 quarts water

2 pounds red beets, trimmed

Sour cream, for serving

Chopped fresh dill, for serving

Season the beef cheeks all over with ½ teaspoon each salt and pepper. Heat the butter in a large heavy pot over medium heat until hot. Sear the beef cheeks, turning once, until browned, about 8 minutes total. Transfer the beef cheeks to a plate. Add the celery and onions to the pan, and cook, stirring occasionally until golden, about 6 minutes. Stir in the caraway seeds and cook until fragrant, about 1 minute. Return the beef cheeks, along with any juices that have collected on the plate, to the pot. Add the water and ¾ teaspoon salt. Bring the liquid to a simmer, skimming off any dark foam, then simmer until the beef cheeks are very tender, about 3½ hours. Transfer the beef cheeks to a cutting board and finely shred, then return the meat to the pot.

Meanwhile, preheat the oven to 425°F.

Place the beets on a large sheet of aluminum foil and season generously with salt. Wrap the foil around the beets to form a package. Roast the beets in the oven until very tender, about 1¼ hours. Let the beets cool slightly, then slip off and discard their skins. Finely chop the beets and add to the pot. Bring the borscht to a simmer and season with salt and pepper to taste. Serve, topped with a dollop of sour cream and some chopped dill.

THE BUTCHER BLOCK

Beef, because of its size, is a great animal for seam cutting, an artisanal technique in which we follow the natural lines of connective tissue to separate the individual muscles. Once you get good enough, you'll need a knife only to remove silver skin and bones; the seams between the muscles can be pulled apart, mostly by hand, making the process of breaking down an animal even more intimate.

Seam cutting is very labor intensive compared to conventional butchering, which uses a bandsaw to slice through muscles and bone. A real disadvantage of box cutting is that it usually includes more than one muscle in a cut. Each muscle cooks slightly differently, depending on how it was used, so if a single cut contains several different muscles, some areas will cook more quickly than others, some areas will be tougher or more tender than others, and so on. Cooking only one muscle (or a piece of one muscle) at a time gives you much more control in the kitchen. And without seam cutting, we would miss out on some of the most delicious cuts of beef, like the petite tender, a muscle in the chuck blade that is one of the most tender in the whole animal. You rarely see it at a butcher counter because it takes some skill to extract and can only be done by this age-old technique. —*Alexi*

FRENCH ONION SOUP

Don't rush cooking the onions here—their deep caramelization is the backbone of this classic soup.

SERVES 6 TO 8

1 tablespoon rendered animal fat or vegetable oil

2½ pounds beef cheeks

Fine sea salt and freshly ground black pepper

4 carrots, chopped

2 celery ribs, chopped

4 thyme sprigs

1 bay leaf

2½ to 3 quarts water

4 tablespoons unsalted butter

2½ pounds onions, thinly sliced

1 tablespoon all-purpose flour

1 cup dry white wine

6 to 8 (½-inch-thick) diagonal slices of baguette, toasted

8 ounces grated Gruyère cheese

2 tablespoons finely grated Parmigiano Reggiano

Heat the fat in a large heavy pot over medium-high heat until hot. Season the beef with ¾ teaspoon salt and ½ teaspoon pepper, then sear, turning once, until browned, about 8 minutes total. Add the carrots, celery, thyme, and bay leaf to the pot then add enough water to cover the meat. Simmer, skimming any foam, until the meat is very tender, 3 to 3½ hours. Remove from the heat and let cool completely. Finely shred the beef. Strain the stock into a bowl, discarding the solids.

Heat the butter in a large heavy pot over medium-high heat. Add the onions and ½ teaspoon salt and cook, stirring frequently and reducing the heat as necessary, until the onions are very soft and deep golden brown, about 45 minutes. Stir in the flour, then add the wine and bring to a boil. Stir in 6 cups of the reserved stock along with the shredded beef. Season with salt and bring to a simmer.

Preheat the broiler. Divide the soup among flameproof bowls, then top with a toasted baguette slice. Stir the cheeses together and sprinkle evenly over the bread. Broil the soup until the cheese is melted and browned, 2 to 3 minutes. Serve very hot.

SHORT RIB RAGU
with Candied Orange and Oil-Cured Olives

We can describe this dish with just three words: Crazy. Deep. Umami. This intense ragu is perfumed with the caramel sweetness of preserved oranges and marjoram (oregano's undersung cousin). On paper, it might seem an unlikely marriage, but there's no arguing against each perfect bite.

SERVES 6 TO 8

1 tablespoon rendered animal fat or vegetable oil

3 pounds bone-in beef short ribs

Fine sea salt and freshly ground black pepper

2 carrots, chopped

2 celery ribs, chopped

1 onion, chopped

1 garlic clove, chopped

4 ounces dried or fresh shiitake mushroom stems

3 cups Rich Beef Stock (page 248)

3 tablespoons all-purpose flour

8 cups whey (page 240)

⅓ cup chopped oil-cured olives

2 tablespoons chopped Candied Valencia Oranges, with some syrup (page 237)

1 pound fresh Pappardelle (page 207)

¼ cup fresh marjoram leaves

Heat the fat in a large heavy pot over medium-high heat until hot. Season the short ribs all over with 1 teaspoon salt and ½ teaspoon pepper. Working in batches if necessary, brown the ribs on all sides, 8 to 10 minutes total. Transfer the ribs to a platter.

Add the carrot, celery, onion, garlic, and mushrooms stems to the pot, scraping up any browned bits, and cook, stirring occasionally, until golden, about 8 minutes. Stir in 1 cup of the beef stock and boil until completely reduced, about 5 minutes. Stir in a second cup of the beef stock and boil until completely reduced, about 5 minutes. Stir in the remaining 1 cup beef stock and reduce completely again.

Sprinkle the flour over the vegetables in the pot. Add the ribs back to the pot along with any accumulated juices and cover with the whey. Bring to a simmer then

cover and simmer gently until the meat is very tender, 3½ to 4 hours. Remove from the heat, uncover, and let the ribs cool completely in the braising liquid.

Remove the ribs from the pot and shred the meat, discarding the bones and any tough membranes. Pour the braising liquid through a fine-mesh sieve set over a medium heavy pot, pressing on and discarding the solids. Add the shredded meat to the pot and bring to a simmer. Stir in the olives and candied oranges.

Cook the pappardelle in boiling salted water until al dente, then drain. Toss the pasta with the ragu, season with salt and pepper to taste, and serve sprinkled with the marjoram leaves.

SLOW-ROASTED BEEF CHUCK EYE ROUND

Low and slow is the way to go with lean cuts like chuck eye round. This easygoing roasting method produces an even, rosy color. But the real shocker here is the sauce, made by reducing whey until it becomes deeply caramelized—think savory dulce de leche. If you don't make your own ricotta (and therefore are low on whey), you can substitute unsalted chicken stock. The resulting sauce will be different but still wonderful. When we feel like going all out, we serve thin slices of this beef topped with some crunchy fleur de sel and a scattering of Roasted Brussels Sprouts (page 77), Twice-Cooked Sunchokes (page 75), and Pickled Red Onions (page 225). Stuff any leftovers into a sandwich with a smear of Horseradish-Mustard Cream (page 215).

SERVES 8 TO 12

1 (5-pound) beef chuck eye round

Fine sea salt

4 large onions (about 2 pounds), sliced

2 heads garlic, cloves crushed

2 tablespoons rendered animal fat or unsalted butter

2 carrots, finely chopped

6 cups whey (page 240)

1 tablespoon water

1½ teaspoons cornstarch

3 tablespoons unsalted butter

Rub the beef all over with 1 tablespoon salt, then place on a rack set inside a roasting pan and refrigerate overnight. Let the beef sit at room temperature for 1 hour before roasting.

Preheat the oven to 200°F.

Scatter the onions and garlic in the bottom of the roasting pan, then place the beef (still on the rack) on top. Place a large piece of parchment paper over the beef, tucking the edges of the paper down around the beef. Cover the pan tightly with aluminum foil and roast in the oven until the beef registers 120°F on an instant-read thermometer, 1 to 1¼ hours. Remove the roast from the oven and transfer to a work surface to rest, 1 hour. Increase the oven temperature to 475°F.

While the beef rests, strain the onions, garlic and any juices in the roasting pan through a fine-mesh sieve set over a bowl. Reserve the jus, discarding the solids.

Heat the rendered fat in a large heavy skillet over medium-high heat until hot. Add the carrots and cook, stirring occasionally, until golden, about 6 minutes. Stir in 1 cup of the whey and boil until the liquid is completely reduced and beginning to caramelize, about 6 minutes. Continue adding the remaining whey, 1 cup at a time, and boil until the whey is completely reduced and caramelized. Add the reserved jus and bring to a simmer. Stir together the water and cornstarch, then stir into the sauce and simmer until thickened, about 1 minute. Whisk the butter, 1 tablespoon at a time, into the sauce then remove the skillet from the heat. Pour the sauce through the cleaned fine-mesh sieve into a bowl, season with salt and pepper, and keep warm.

Place the beef on a baking sheet and brown in the oven until the surface of the meat is lightly browned, about 15 minutes. Transfer the beef to a work surface and slice thinly. Serve with the reserved sauce.

TWICE-COOKED SUNCHOKES

Lightly smashing parboiled sunchokes (sometimes called Jerusalem artichokes) before frying them increases their surface area and creates lots of crags and jags that crisp up beautifully in the hot fat.

SERVES 6 TO 8

2 pounds sunchokes

Fine sea salt

About 4 cups rendered animal fat or vegetable oil

EQUIPMENT: **A deep-fry or candy thermometer**

Place the sunchokes in a medium saucepan and cover with water by 1 inch. Stir in 2 teaspoons salt then bring to a boil. Reduce the heat and simmer until the sunchokes are tender, about 15 minutes. Strain the sunchokes and let cool slightly.

Heat the oil in a large deep heavy skillet over medium heat to 400°F. Using a large heavy spatula, gently smash the sunchokes, taking care to keep each in one piece. Fry the sunchokes in batches, until golden and crisp, about 8 minutes per batch. Transfer the sunchokes to a paper towel–lined platter and sprinkle with salt. Serve immediately.

ROASTED BRUSSELS SPROUTS

Sometimes it's our job in the kitchen to just not mess things up. Roasty, browned Brussels sprouts need no embellishment and always hit the spot.

SERVES 6 TO 8

2 pounds Brussels sprouts, trimmed and halved

2 garlic cloves, finely chopped

2 tablespoons extra-virgin olive oil

Fine sea salt and freshly ground black pepper

Preheat the oven to 425°F.

Toss the Brussels sprouts with the garlic, olive oil, ½ teaspoon salt, and ¼ teaspoon pepper. Spread the Brussels sprouts on 2 baking sheets then roast in the oven, stirring once and rotating the pans, until golden brown, about 40 minutes.

WINE AND VINEGAR–BRAISED BEEF TONGUE

An underused cut that becomes almost silky when braised, beef tongue is a favorite of ours. Pig's blood helps thicken the sauce and adds fathoms of deep, almost chocolatey flavor. We love this with Mashed Potatoes (page 80), Glazed Carrots and Fiddlehead Ferns (page 81), and a scattering of sharp watercress.

SERVES 6 TO 8

1 (1½- to 2-pound) fresh beef tongue

1 (750ml) bottle dry red wine

½ cup red wine vinegar

1 onion, chopped

1 carrot, chopped

1 celery rib, chopped, or ¼ cup finely chopped celery root

Fine sea salt

2 tablespoons rendered animal fat or unsalted butter

2 garlic cloves, smashed

1 rosemary sprig

8 cups Rich Beef, Chicken, or Pork stock, or as needed (pages 245-248)

1 cup pig's blood

6 tablespoons unsalted butter

Place the tongue in a pot just big enough to hold it then add the wine, vinegar, onion, carrot, and celery (the tongue should be fully submerged in the wine mixture). Cover the pot and refrigerate for 2 days.

Transfer the tongue to a work surface and pat dry. Sprinkle the tongue evenly with 1 teaspoon salt and let stand at room temperature for 1 hour.

Pour the marinade through a fine-mesh sieve, reserving both the vegetables and the liquid. Wipe the pot dry.

Preheat the oven to 350°F.

Heat the rendered fat in the dried pot over medium-high heat until hot. Stir in the reserved vegetables from the marinade and cook, stirring occasionally, until well browned, about 8 minutes. Stir in 1 cup of the reserved marinating liquid and boil to reduce it completely, about 6 minutes. Let the bottom of the pot begin to brown, then add another cup of the reserved liquid, reducing it in the same manner and stirring

occasionally. Add the remaining reserved liquid and reduce until the liquid measures about ¼ cup.

Return the tongue to the pot, along with the garlic and rosemary. Add enough stock to just cover the tongue and bring to a simmer. Cover the pot tightly with aluminum foil and a lid, then braise in the oven until the tongue is very tender, 3½ to 4 hours. Transfer the tongue to a work surface and let cool slightly.

Strain the braising liquid through a fine-mesh sieve, discarding the solids. Bring the liquid to a boil and cook until reduced by half. Lower the heat so that the liquid is at a bare simmer. Pulse the blood in a blender until smooth and liquefied, then whisk the blood into the barely simmering sauce. Simmer until thickened, about 2 minutes. Transfer the sauce to a blender, add the butter, and blend until smooth and emulsified (use caution when blending hot liquids). Season the sauce with salt to taste. Keep the sauce warm until ready to use.

Peel and discard the skin from the tongue, then cut the tongue crosswise into 1-inch-thick slices. Serve the tongue with the reserved sauce.

MASHED POTATOES

Salt-roasting is a great way to increase the natural flavor of potatoes. It also helps keep their flesh dry and fluffy, which lets them soak up more cream and butter when mashed.

SERVES 6 TO 8

2 pounds Yukon Gold potatoes

¼ cup coarse sea salt

½ cup heavy cream

2 tablespoons unsalted butter

Fine sea salt

Preheat the oven to 425°F.

Place the potatoes on a baking sheet, then sprinkle with the coarse salt. Roast the potatoes until tender, about 1 hour. Let stand until just cool enough to handle, then peel.

Place the potatoes in a large bowl. Add the cream and butter and mash together to the desired texture. Season to taste with salt, gently reheat if necessary, and serve.

GLAZED CARROTS AND FIDDLEHEAD FERNS

With their glossy mouthfeel and gentle sweetness, glazed carrots always satisfy, and a handful of fiddlehead ferns keeps things interesting. Substitute lima beans for the fiddleheads later in the season.

SERVES 6 TO 8

2 tablespoons rendered animal fat or unsalted butter

1 pound carrots, cut into coins

¼ pound fiddlehead ferns, cleaned

Fine sea salt and freshly ground black pepper

2 cups Rich Chicken Stock (page 246)

2 tablespoons Grade B maple syrup

2 teaspoons Pickled Mustard Seeds (page 212)

Heat the rendered fat in a large heavy skillet over medium-high heat until hot. Add the carrots and fiddleheads and season with ½ teaspoon salt and ¼ teaspoon pepper. Cook, stirring occasionally, until golden, about 6 minutes. Reduce the heat to medium low, then add the stock. Cover the skillet and cook until the carrots are tender, about 12 minutes. Uncover the skillet and stir in the maple syrup and pickled mustard seeds, then increase the heat to high and cook, stirring occasionally, until the liquid is reduced to a glaze, about 4 minutes. Season with salt and pepper to taste, then serve.

NERVETTI SALAD

It takes a little doing to transform an otherwise inedible beef scrap into a highly praised dish. While it's true that this dish takes a week to prepare from start to finish, most of that time is hands off, as the tendons soak and tenderize in various solutions of acid, sugar, and salt. Finally, a long poach in a sprightly court bouillon transforms these "nerves" into translucent noodles. We usually serve this salad over slices of perfectly ripe tomatoes, but it would make a fine addition to a Vietnamese bánh mì, tucked into French bread and showered with fresh cilantro and mint.

SERVES 10 TO 12

½ cup red wine vinegar

1½ pounds beef tendons, about 1¼ inches in diameter

Fine sea salt

4 quarts Heavy Brine (page 249)

2 onions, quartered

2 carrots, chopped

2 celery ribs, chopped

½ cup Dehydrated Sweet Peppers (page 239)

1 bunch parsley

1 bunch thyme

1 bunch sage

½ cup apple cider vinegar

2 cups finely chopped Giardiniera (page 219)

1 cup mixed chopped fresh herbs, such as cilantro and mint or parsley, basil, and oregano

2 to 3 large ripe tomatoes

Chile Oil (page 234)

Combine the red wine vinegar with 6 cups water in a large bowl. Add the tendons and soak, chilled, for 24 hours. Drain the tendons.

Combine 1 tablespoon salt with 6 cups fresh warm water, stirring until the salt is dissolved. Add the tendons and soak, chilled, for 24 hours. Drain the tendons.

Pour the brine into the cleaned bowl and add the tendons. Soak, chilled, for 48 hours. Drain the tendons.

Combine the onions, carrots, celery, dehydrated sweet peppers, parsley, thyme, sage, apple cider vinegar, and 2 teaspoons salt with 3 quarts water in a heavy pot. Submerge the tendons in the court bouillon and place over low heat. Bring the liquid to 180°F and keep the mixture at 180°F until the tendons are tender and translucent, but not falling apart, about 8 hours (use a candy or deep-fry thermometer to regulate the temperature). Chill the tendons in the court bouillon until cold.

Transfer the tendons to a cutting board (save the court bouillon for making soup, if you like) and cut into 2-inch lengths. Slice the tendons as thinly as possible, then julienne into noodles. Toss the tendon noodles with the giardiniera and chopped herbs then season to taste with salt.

To serve, slice the tomatoes thickly and arrange on a serving plate. Top the tomato slices with the nervetti salad, then drizzle with the chile oil.

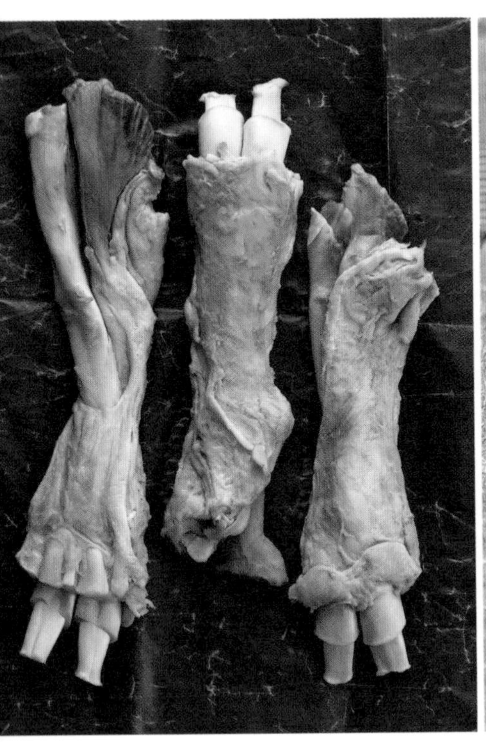

Beef tendons await their transformation into nervetti salad; two Devons pick their way across Wyebrook Farm's grassy pasture above the restaurant.

GINGERED RHUBARB CROSTATA
with Double-Fat Crust

Rhubarb and ginger are happy bedfellows, especially when nestled up in this exceptionally flaky crust, made with a combination of beef suet and butter.

SERVES 8

FOR THE CRUST

½ cup beef suet, cut into ½-inch pieces and frozen

4 tablespoons unsalted butter, cut into ½-inch pieces and frozen

1 cup all-purpose flour

Fine sea salt

4 to 5 tablespoons cold water

FOR THE FILLING

12 ounces rhubarb, cut into ½-inch pieces

1 cup granulated sugar

1 tablespoon finely chopped fresh ginger

1½ teaspoons cornstarch

1 teaspoon vanilla

1 egg, beaten with a pinch of salt

1 tablespoon demerara sugar

Make the crust: Grate the frozen suet and butter using a food processor fit with the grater blade. Change out the grater blade for the chopping blade.

Add the flour and ¼ teaspoon salt to the food processor, pulsing until the fat is mostly combined but still has some small lumps. Stir in 3 tablespoons of the water with a fork then squeeze a small handful of the dough. If it is still crumbly, add the remaining water, 1 tablespoon at a time, until the dough just comes together. Pat the dough into a round, then wrap it in plastic wrap and chill at least 1 hour.

Preheat the oven to 400°F. Roll the dough out on a floured work surface with a floured rolling pin into a 14-inch round. Transfer the dough to a buttered baking sheet.

Combine the rhubarb, granulated sugar, ginger, cornstarch, and vanilla. Spread the filling evenly over the dough, leaving a 1½-inch border. Fold the edge of the dough over the filling, overlapping it as needed. Brush the dough with some of the egg wash then sprinkle with the demerara sugar. Bake the crostata until the filling is bubbling and the pastry is golden, 30 to 40 minutes.

A FARM FEAST MENU FOR SPRING

The day I met Dean, he took me to the woods where his pigs forage. As animals rooted around us, we sat on a downed tree and talked about his vision for the farm. I was immediately taken. He was raising old breeds once prized for their fat and flavor, including the Ossabaw, which he sold me for a pig roast. People are still talking about that pig—its skin shattered like glass, and the meat was almost the color of beef.

A year later, Dean invited me to be a guest chef at Wyebrook. He sent me a list of available meats and suggested I cook at least six courses, but those were his only guidelines. To be handed the best quality products and given unlimited creative freedom is a cook's dream come true. It seems this is just the way Dean operates. He finds people he likes, gives them the resources they need, and lets them run with it.

It was late spring when I arrived at the farm. I spent several days in the kitchen and noticed that Wyebrook's staff is not like other restaurants'. These people are happy. They gaze across the cooking line out to the old barnyard, now a comfortable space filled with picnic tables and musicians playing bluegrass. These cooks get to work with the best stuff around, then watch as it gets devoured by dancing guests. They have it good, and they know it.

I knew it, too. I was having fun dreaming up the dishes, but one in particular stood out to me and to the guests—the goat rillettes. I seared squares of the confited meat and served it with toasted sweet corn, a Pennsylvania Dutch staple. Rillettes is the French name for this dish, but around here, we call it scrapple. I explained this fine difference of provenance to the guests at the feast. Some moaned when they heard the word scrapple, but I wasn't surprised when it turned out to be the hands-down favorite of the evening.

There is a lesson here. We look at the local traditions in this country as staid or even frumpy (and certainly there are cases where that is true), but if the only difference between a delicious rillettes and a delicious scrapple is where it is grown and made, perhaps we should look at some of our other food traditions with new eyes. That gets a whole lot easier when the local ingredients we use are of such admirable quality. —*Ian*

SPRING RADISHES
with Bacon Butter

We could wax on and on about the complexity and finesse of this compound butter, but really, the name says it all: Bacon Butter. Serve it with radishes in the spring and homemade bread all year long.

SERVES 8

¼ pound bacon, finely chopped

2 teaspoons coriander seeds, crushed

½ cup (1 stick) unsalted butter, softened

1 shallot, finely chopped

1 teaspoon finely grated lemon zest

1 tablespoon lemon juice

1 teaspoon finely chopped fresh thyme

Fine sea salt and freshly ground black pepper

4 bunches radishes, trimmed with some greens attached

Cook the bacon in a large heavy skillet over medium heat, stirring occasionally, until golden, about 8 minutes. Add the coriander and cook, stirring, for 1 minute. Transfer the bacon mixture to the bowl of an electric mixer and let cool to room temperature.

Add the butter, shallot, lemon zest, juice, thyme, and ¼ teaspoon each salt and pepper to the bacon mixture and beat with the mixer until pale and fluffy, about 3 minutes. Season to taste with salt and pepper. Serve with the radishes.

POACHED BABY VEGETABLES IN GELÉE

Slender purple carrots, golden beets, and zucchini suspended in a delicate gelée form a beautiful mosaic. Make this when you can find pristine baby vegetables at the farm or local markets, or in your own garden.

SERVES 8

2½ pounds baby golden beets (1 to 2 inches in diameter)

Fine sea salt and freshly ground black pepper

2½ pounds baby purple carrots

2 tablespoons extra-virgin olive oil

2 large leeks

2 medium orange carrots, peeled and chopped

2 celery ribs, chopped

2 shallots, chopped

2 cups dry white wine

10 black peppercorns

3¼ cups cold water

2 pounds baby zucchini, trimmed

4½ teaspoons powdered unflavored gelatin

½ cup chopped mixed tender fresh herbs, such as basil and chervil

1 bunch fresh chives, chopped

¼ cup Lemon-Infused Olive Oil (page 234), for serving

Fleur de sel, for serving

1 cup assorted micro greens, for serving

EQUIPMENT: **A (6- to 8-cup) terrine mold or loaf pan**

Preheat the oven to 450°F.

Trim the beets, leaving ½ inch of the stems intact. Place the beets on a large sheet of aluminum foil and season generously with salt. Wrap the foil around the beets to form a package. Roast on a baking sheet until very tender, 1 to 1½ hours. Let the beets cool for 15 minutes, then slip off and discard their skins, and cut the beets into 1-inch wedges if large or keep whole if very small. Season the beets with salt and pepper.

While the beets roast, peel the purple carrots and toss with the olive oil, ½ teaspoon salt, and ¼ teaspoon pepper, then place on baking sheets and roast until tender, about 30 minutes. Let the carrots cool.

While the beets and carrots roast, coarsely chop the leeks, then wash well, and transfer to a stockpot. Add the orange carrots, celery, shallots, wine, peppercorns, 1 teaspoon salt, and 3 cups cold water. Bring to a boil then reduce the heat and simmer, uncovered, for 30 minutes.

Pour the stock through a fine-mesh sieve into a bowl, discarding the solids. Return the stock to the cleaned stockpot. Add the zucchini, bring to a gentle simmer, and cook until tender, about 8 minutes. Transfer the zucchini to a work surface and measure the stock. If the stock measures more than 2½ cups, boil until reduced to 2½ cups. If there is less, add enough water to measure 2½ cups. Season to taste with salt and pepper.

Stir the gelatin into the remaining ¼ cup cold water and let stand 1 minute to soften, then add to the hot stock, stirring until dissolved. Set aside.

Lightly oil the terrine mold then line the long sides and bottom with a sheet of plastic wrap, smoothing out any wrinkles and allowing at least 2 inches of overhang on each side. Pour about ½ cup of the gelatin mixture into the terrine and chill it until just set.

Lay the zucchini lengthwise over the set gelatin layer. Sprinkle with a third of the chopped herbs and chives. Make a layer of beets over the zucchini, and sprinkle with a third of the chopped herbs and chives. Lay the purple carrots on top and sprinkle with the remaining chopped herbs and chives.

Stir the remaining gelatin mixture then pour in all but ½ cup (reserve the remainder at room temperature), gently pushing down the vegetables so they are just covered by the gelatin mixture. Chill, uncovered, until top is set, 1½ to 2 hours.

If the reserved ½ cup gelatin mixture has begun to set, heat it until it is just liquefied but not hot, then pour over the set terrine. Chill until firm, about 2 hours.

To serve, invert the terrine onto a cutting board, gently pulling on the overhanging plastic wrap to help unmold it (discard the plastic wrap). Carefully slice the terrine with a very sharp serrated knife. Transfer the slices to serving plates. Drizzle some lemon-infused olive oil around the plates, sprinkle fleur de sel and coarsely ground black pepper over the terrine, and garnish with the micro greens.

Spring at Wyebrook is a riot of greens and fresh flavors, a welcome antidote to the gray months of a long mid-Atlantic winter.

GRILLED BEEF TONGUE
with Spring Herb Chimichurri

With its sumptuous texture and lush flavor, beef tongue may be the most undersung of all the animal's parts. Bonus: It's very easy to cook. Bright, herbaceous chimichurri sauce, traditionally served with South American–style grilled beef, cuts the meat's richness. Hold on to that flavorful cooking liquid for making soup down the road.

SERVES 8

FOR THE TONGUE

1 (1½- to 2-pound) beef tongue

2 carrots, peeled

2 celery ribs

1 large onion, unpeeled and quartered

1 head garlic, halved crosswise

1 small bunch flat-leaf parsley

6 thyme sprigs

2 bay leaves

2 teaspoons black peppercorns

Fine sea salt

2 tablespoons rendered animal fat or unsalted butter, melted

1 cup watercress, for serving

FOR THE CHIMICHURRI

Leaves from 1 bunch cilantro

Leaves from 1 bunch flat-leaf parsley

1 bunch chives

¼ cup lavender leaves

2 garlic cloves, chopped

¼ cup red-wine vinegar

1 cup extra-virgin olive oil

Fine sea salt and freshly ground black pepper

Cook the tongue: Place the tongue in a stockpot with the carrots, celery, onion, garlic, parsley, thyme, bay leaves, peppercorns, and 2 teaspoons salt. Add enough water to cover the tongue, then bring to a simmer over medium to medium-low heat. Gently simmer, skimming away any dark foam from the surface, until the tongue is very tender, about 4 hours. Remove from the heat and cool slightly.

While the tongue simmers, make the chimichurri: Coarsely chop the cilantro, parsley, chives, and lavender and place in a blender with the garlic and vinegar. With the motor

running, pour the oil into the blender in a stream, blending until finely puréed. Season the chimichurri with salt and pepper to taste, and set aside.

Preheat a grill, preferably with hardwood or hardwood charcoal.

Remove the tongue from the liquid (save for another use, if you like) and pat dry. Peel and discard the skin from the tongue. Cut the tongue diagonally into ½-inch-thick slices.

Brush the tongue slices with the melted fat and season with salt and pepper. Grill the tongue slices, turning once, until grill marks appear, about 6 minutes total. Serve the tongue with the chimichurri and watercress.

GOAT RILLETTES

with Pennsylvania Chile Sauce

Rillettes, the French name that describes this confit, can be made with any type of shredded meat. The Pennsylvania Dutch use pork and beef to make a similar dish, thickened with cornmeal, called scrapple. When served with Stewed Toasted Sweet Corn (page 102) and a chile sauce made from local peppers, it becomes neither French nor Pennsylvania Dutch, but something completely new.

SERVES 8 TO 12

3½ to 4 pounds bone-in goat shoulder and neck

Fine sea salt and freshly ground black pepper

12 garlic cloves, peeled

1 bunch fresh thyme

4 bay leaves

3 to 4 quarts rendered animal fats in any combination, such as pork, chicken and/or beef, melted

Stewed Toasted Sweet Corn (page 102)

Pennsylvania Chile Sauce (page 233)

⅓ cup crumbled fresh farmer's cheese or queso fresco, for serving

Small sprouts, such as beet or Swiss chard, for serving

Preheat the oven to 375°F.

Cut the goat into pieces at the joints, or have a butcher do this for you. Season the meat with 1½ teaspoons salt and ½ teaspoon pepper, then place in a deep baking dish. Scatter the garlic, thyme, and bay leaves around the meat. Add enough melted fat to completely cover the meat, then tightly cover the dish with aluminum foil. Bake until the meat is very tender and falling off the bone, about 3½ hours. Remove the dish from the oven and let cool slightly. Discard the bay leaves and thyme, then remove the meat and garlic from the fat. Reserve the fat for another use.

Shred the meat into a bowl then, using your hands, mash the garlic into the meat. Pulse half of the meat mixture in a food processor until finely ground. Mix the ground meat back into the shredded meat. Season the meat with salt and pepper to taste. Spread the rillettes evenly onto an 11 x 17-inch baking sheet, gently packing it down and smoothing it. Chill until set, about 4 hours.

Using a sharp knife, cut the rillettes into 3-inch squares. Heat a dry large cast-iron griddle or skillet over medium-high heat until hot. Sear the rillettes, turning once, until crisp and golden brown, 6 to 8 minutes total. Serve the rillettes with the toasted sweet corn, chile sauce, and cheese, garnished with the sprouts.

STEWED TOASTED SWEET CORN

The toasty sweetness of dried corn is a staple around Pennsylvania Dutch tables and has traditionally been a way to preserve the summer harvest for use throughout the year.

SERVES 8 TO 12

2 cups toasted dried sweet corn, such as Cope's

3 cups boiling water

3 cups whole milk

3 tablespoons unsalted butter

1 tablespoon sugar

Fine sea salt and freshly ground black pepper

1 cup heavy cream

Place the corn in a large heavy pot and stir in the boiling water. Let the corn soak for at least 2 hours, then transfer the pot to the stovetop, stir in the milk, and bring to a simmer. Add the butter, sugar, and ¾ teaspoon salt and cook, stirring more frequently as the mixture thickens, until the corn is tender, about 45 minutes. Stir in the cream and season to taste with salt and pepper.

PORK LOIN
with Ramp Butter, Sugar Snaps, and Pea Shoots

The pork loins at Wyebrook come with a thick layer of fat on one side that crisps as it roasts. Opening up this loin jellyroll-style and filling it with ramp butter is a way to marble the rest of the loin with bright spring flavor.

SERVES 6 TO 8

6 ounces ramps or scallions

6 tablespoons unsalted butter

Fine sea salt and freshly ground black pepper

1 (4-pound) boneless pork loin, preferably with fat cap attached

2 tablespoons coriander seeds

1 bay leaf

1 pound sugar snap peas, trimmed and sliced diagonally

1 cup pea shoots

Carrot Miso Purée, for serving

Finely chop the ramp whites and cut the greens into 1-inch pieces. Heat 3 tablespoons butter in a heavy skillet over medium heat until hot. Stir in the ramps and ½ teaspoon salt and cook, stirring until tender, about 5 minutes. Transfer the mixture to a food processor and pulse until finely chopped. Reserve the ramp butter.

Preheat the oven to 400°F.

Place the pork loin on a work surface, fat side down, and cut a 1-inch-deep incision along the length of the loin, about a quarter of the way in. Open the incision, laying the fat-side flush with the work surface. Make additional 1-inch-deep incisions, opening up and unrolling the loin as you cut until it is flattened in an even layer. Season the loin with a generous pinch each of salt and pepper. Spread the ramp butter evenly over the meat then roll the loin back up like a jelly roll. Tie the loin at 2-inch intervals with kitchen string so that it holds its original shape.

Grind the coriander seeds and bay leaf to a powder in a spice grinder. Stir in 1 teaspoon salt and ½ teaspoon pepper, then rub the spice mixture all over the loin.

Place the loin in a roasting pan and roast until an instant-read thermometer registers 135°F, 45 minutes to 1 hour. Let the meat stand at room temperature for 15 minutes before slicing.

Place a steamer insert over a pot of boiling water, then add the snap peas and cook, covered, until bright green and crisp-tender, about 5 minutes. Transfer the snap peas to a large bowl and toss with the remaining 3 tablespoons butter and salt to taste. Serve the sliced pork loin with the snap peas, pea shoots, and the carrot miso purée.

CARROT-MISO PURÉE

Miso adds depth and intriguing sweetness to almost any vegetable purée. Try it with rutabaga, turnips, or celery root.

SERVES 6 TO 8

2 pounds carrots, chopped

Fine sea salt and freshly ground black pepper

¼ cup white miso

4 tablespoons unsalted butter

Place the carrots in a saucepan and cover with water by 2 inches. Stir in 1 teaspoon salt and bring to a boil. Boil the carrots until very tender, about 30 minutes. Using a slotted spoon, transfer the carrots to a blender along with the miso, butter, and 1 to 2 tablespoons of the carrot cooking water. Purée until very smooth. Season the purée with salt and pepper to taste.

HONEY PANNA COTTA

Here's a little trick to make a good panna cotta into something ethereal: Reserve some of the cream and whip it before folding it into the rest of the gelatin mixture. This leaves you with a texture that is surprisingly light on the tongue. Use whatever fruit is perfectly ripe for this recipe. Depending on the season, it's especially good with rhubarb, blueberries, or sliced peaches.

SERVES 8

3 cups heavy cream

½ cup honey

Fine sea salt

2¼ teaspoons unflavored gelatin

2 tablespoons water

⅓ cup sour cream

¾ cup sugar

¾ cup water

3 cups ripe seasonal fruit, sliced if necessary

EQUIPMENT: **8 (½-cup) ramekins**

Heat 2½ cups of the cream, the honey, and ¼ teaspoon salt in a small saucepan over low heat, stirring until the honey is dissolved, then remove from the heat.

Sprinkle the gelatin over the water in a small bowl and let soften. Whisk the gelatin mixture into the honey cream until dissolved, then whisk in the sour cream. Chill the cream mixture until it has thickened to the consistency of egg whites.

Whip the remaining ½ cup heavy cream until it just holds soft peaks. Fold the whipped cream into the chilled cream mixture then divide between the lightly oiled ramekins. Chill until the panna cottas are set, about 3 hours.

Bring the sugar, water, and a pinch of salt to a boil in a small saucepan. Pour the hot syrup over the fruit, then let cool to room temperature.

To serve, remove the panna cottas from their molds, if you like, and serve with the fruit and syrup.

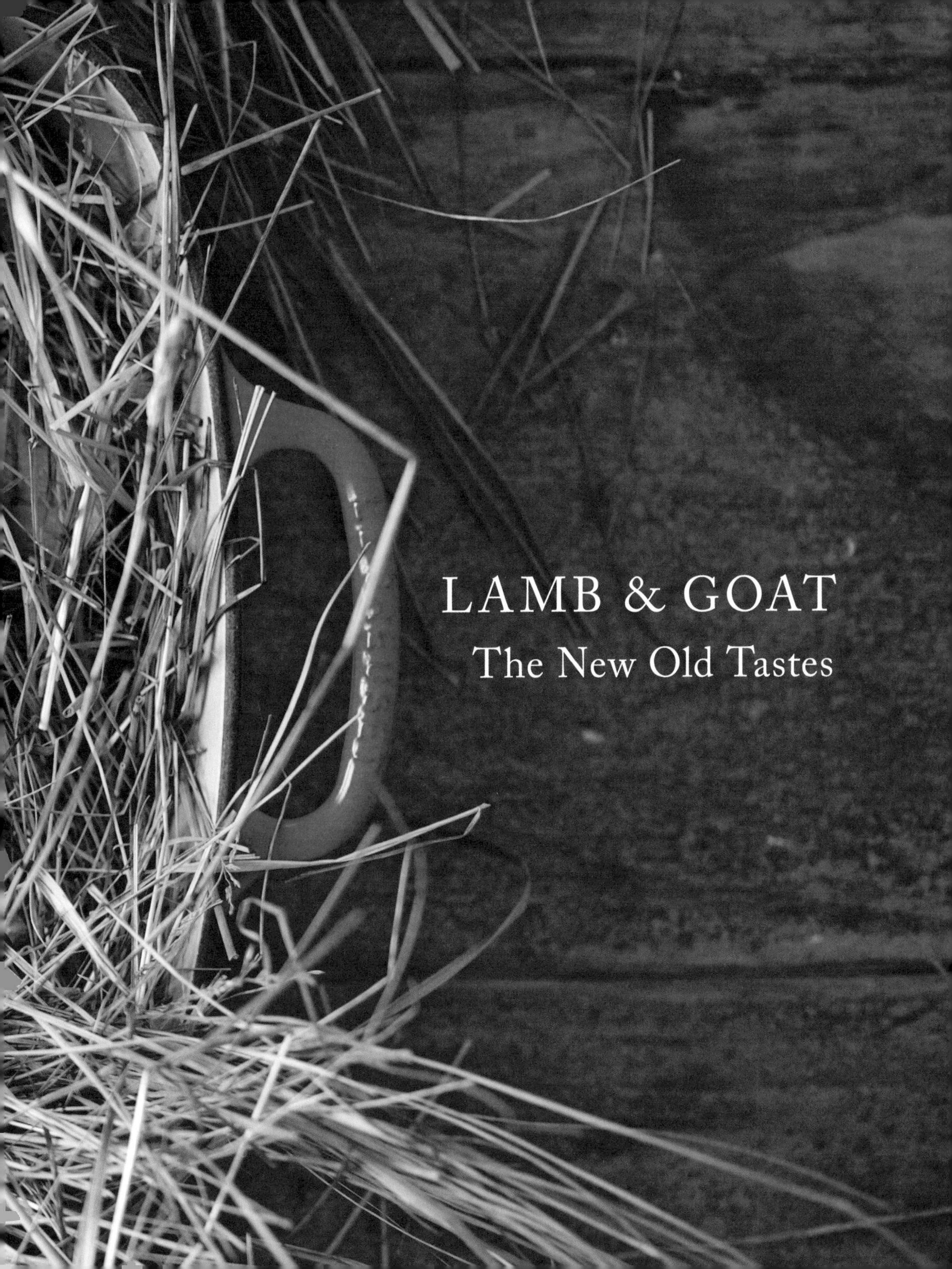

LAMB & GOAT
The New Old Tastes

Grass-fed beef is a wonder to eat. It tastes much cleaner than feedlot beef and, as I've mentioned, is a great way to convert solar energy into caloric energy. Unfortunately, because they require a lot more intake than other animals and need large, open fields to thrive, cattle are fairly inefficient at that process. While we have plenty of pasture land at Wyebrook, there are other animals—namely sheep and goats—that utilize grasses much more efficiently. Both animals are popular around the world as excellent, delicious sources of protein. It's time for them to find a larger audience in the U.S.

Sheep and goats have different styles of grazing. Goats will stand on their hind legs to pluck twigs and leaves from the tops of shrubs. They are agile and cunning and do well in the wooded areas where we keep our pigs. Sheep, on the other hand, graze on grasses and clover. They keep their heads down and mostly mind their own business, munching away. We let them roam in the same fields as the cattle. By alternating the sheep with cattle and the goats with pigs, we are able to extend the grazing on a given amount of land.

We have experimented in the past with buying male goats and sheep from neighboring dairy farms. These animals have done well for us and provided great meat, but now we are turning our focus to breeds that are meant for meat rather than dairy. To that end, we are adding a number of Katahdin sheep and Boer goats to our flocks.

I find it strange that most people in this country are not accustomed to eating lamb or goat. Of all the animals we consume in the U.S., these two rank at the very bottom. Americans just don't know what they're missing, but we're on a mission to change that. The flavor of both lamb and goat is complex and when cooked properly, just outstanding. —*Dean*

SEAR-CRUSTED LEG OF LAMB

Wyebrook's grass-fed lamb has tons of flavor all on its own, and this two-ingredient recipe showcases that natural complexity perfectly. Don't skimp on the searing time—it's the secret to the lamb's crisp outer crust and deep browned flavor. If you do want to dress things up a bit, add a dollop of Salsa Verde (page 116).

SERVES 6 TO 8

1 (2¼- to 2½-pound) piece boneless leg of lamb

Fine sea salt

Lay the lamb out on a work surface. Using a meat pounder, pound the meat into an even layer, about 1¼ inches thick. Sprinkle the lamb evenly with 1 teaspoon salt.

Preheat the oven to 225°F.

Heat a very large dry heavy cast-iron skillet over high heat until hot. Place the lamb in the skillet (it should just fit), and immediately lower the heat to medium. Sear the lamb without moving it, until a thick, brown crust forms, about 15 minutes (the lamb will shrink a bit as it cooks). Flip the lamb and transfer the skillet to the oven. Roast the lamb until an instant-read thermometer registers 125°F, about 10 minutes. Transfer the lamb to a cutting board and let stand for 10 minutes before thinly slicing.

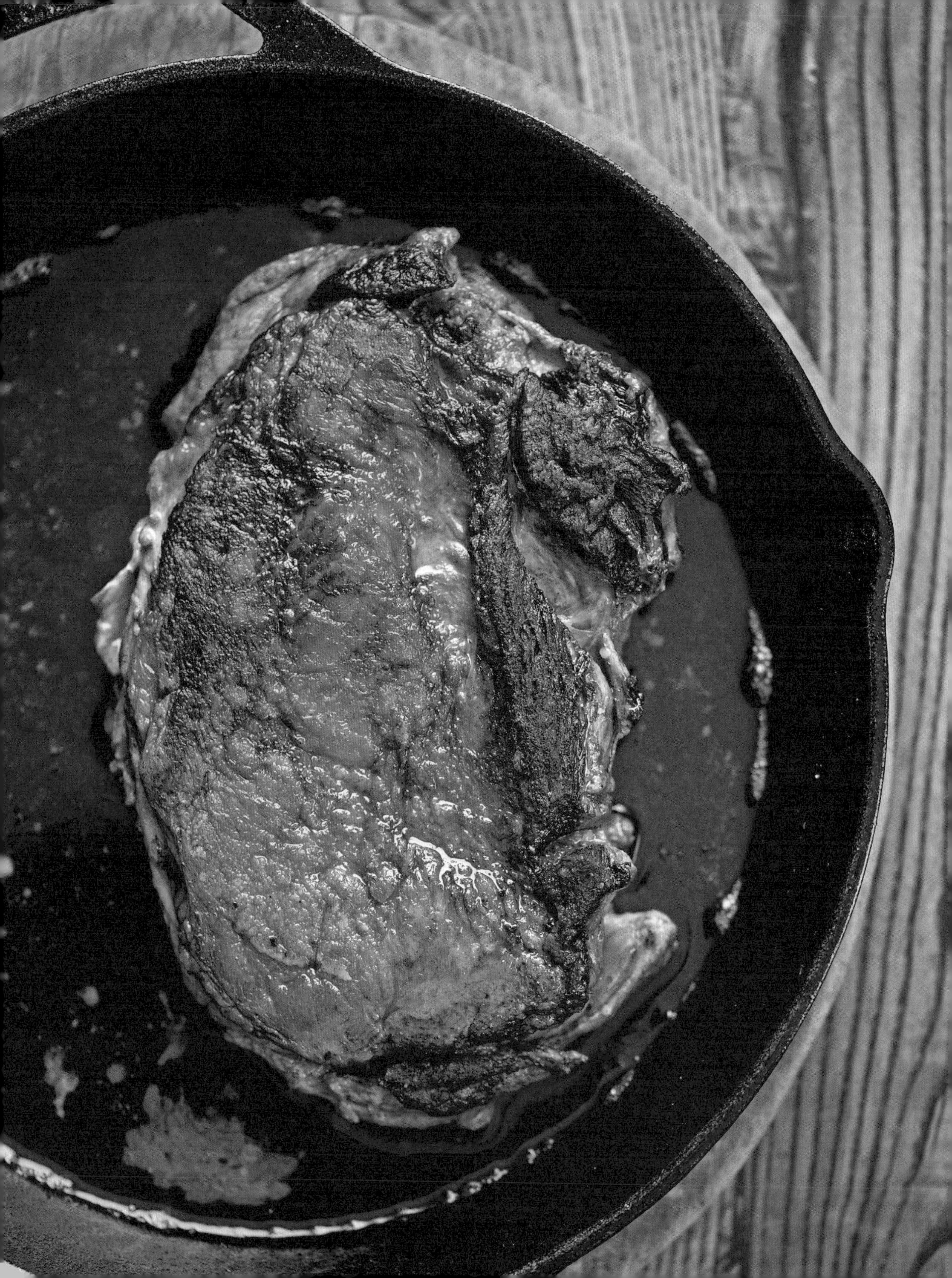

SALSA VERDE

We love this bright sauce with rich, unctuous cuts of meat, like beef tongue, pork belly, and leg of lamb.

MAKES ABOUT 1 QUART

Leaves from 2 bunches flat-leaf parsley

Leaves from 1 bunch cilantro

2 garlic cloves

2 soft boiled eggs, at room temperature

2 tablespoons whole-grain mustard

3 cups extra-virgin olive oil

½ cup red wine vinegar, or to taste

¼ cup capers, drained and coarsely chopped

Fine sea salt

Using a mortar and pestle, grind together the parsley, cilantro, and garlic until finely chopped and combined, about 6 minutes. (Alternatively, pulse the herbs and garlic in a food processor until finely chopped.) Separate the egg yolks from the whites. Add the yolks to the herb mixture and stir until combined. Transfer the mixture to a large bowl.

Finely chop the egg whites, then stir them into the sauce along with the mustard. Slowly whisk in the oil (the slower you whisk in the oil, the more emulsified the sauce will be). Whisk in the vinegar then stir in the capers. Season with 1½ teaspoons salt and additional vinegar to taste. Refrigerated in an airtight container, the salsa will keep for 1 week.

MERGUEZ SAUSAGE

We season our version of this classic North African lamb sausage with ras el hanout, which we make ourselves by combining dried sweet peppers and tomatoes with chiles and spices.

MAKES ABOUT 5 POUNDS

3¾ pounds lamb meat, cut into cubes

1¼ pounds lamb fat trimmings

½ cup Dehydrated Sweet Peppers (page 239)

¼ cup sun-dried tomatoes

3 dried hot chiles, stemmed

2 teaspoons coriander seeds

1 teaspoon cumin seeds

1 teaspoon allspice berries

1 teaspoon black peppercorns

½ teaspoon ground mace

Fine sea salt

About 6 feet of hog casings

EQUIPMENT: **Meat grinder, sausage stuffer, a pin**

Place the lamb and fat trimmings on a baking sheet and put in the freezer until the edges of the meat just start to freeze (the center should remain unfrozen), about 30 minutes.

Combine the dehydrated sweet peppers, sun-dried tomatoes, chiles, coriander, cumin, allspice, peppercorns, and mace in a spice grinder and grind to a powder. In a large bowl, quickly toss together the lamb and fat with the spice mixture and 4 teaspoons salt.

Grind the spiced lamb mixture using a ⅛-inch die on a meat grinder and let it fall into a chilled bowl set over ice.

Using a sausage stuffer, fill the casings with the filling, twisting the casings to make 6- to 8-inch links. Prick each link 2 or 3 times with the pin. Let the sausages hang at cool room temperature for 24 hours. Chill the sausages until ready to cook.

Preheat a grill, preferably with hardwood or hardwood charcoal. Grill the sausages, turning occasionally, until the skin is golden brown but the center is still somewhat pink, about 8 minutes.

SEVEN FIRES–STYLE ROAST LAMB

We have admired Argentine chef Francis Mallmann for years, and his bold cooking style directly inspired this dish. We love to grill out in the barnyard during the summer months, using a gaucho grill and a hardwood-fueled fire. This whole lamb cooks slowly for many hours, filling the farm with the warm waft of sizzling meat—an aroma so intoxicating, we're sure chef Francis would approve.

SERVES 20 TO 30

8 cups water

¼ cup brown sugar

4 dried chiles

4 bay leaves

2 tablespoons coriander seeds

Fine sea salt

1 (30- to 35-pound) whole lamb

3 bunches rosemary, tied together to make a brush

EQUIPMENT: **Hardwood, a shovel, a hacksaw, one 1½-foot length of rebar plus four 4-foot lengths of rebar, heavy-duty fireplace gloves**

Put the water, brown sugar, chiles, bay leaves, coriander, and ¾ cup salt in a medium pot and bring to a simmer, stirring to dissolve the salt. Remove from the heat and let the brine cool to room temperature.

Start a fire with the hardwood in a fire pit or gaucho grill. Use the shovel to move the fire as needed.

Lay the lamb, legs up, on a work surface or paper-lined picnic table. Using the hacksaw, cut through the center of the hip bones and press the hind legs apart. Cut through the breastbone and press down and out on the 2 sides of the rib cage to open the chest cavity. Place the 1½-foot length of rebar crosswise in the chest cavity to keep it opened. Turn the lamb over so it is back side up.

Make an incision between the fourth and fifth ribs on either side of the rib cage. Force one 4-foot piece of rebar crosswise through the incisions. Make an incision through the thickest part of each hind leg, underneath the bone, running parallel to the length of the body and into the cavity. Run a 4-foot piece of rebar through each

Keeping a hard-working farm ready for visitors isn't easy, but the community is invited to see where their meat is raised and butchered.

incision, into the cavity and above the perpendicular rebar. Force the parallel rebars through the opening in the throat and out the mouth to form an A-frame of rebar. Wrap the bottom of the hind legs in aluminum foil (they will rest on the ground). Prop the lamb at a 50 to 55° angle, using the remaining 4-foot piece of rebar as a support.

Using the shovel and fireplace gloves, move the fire closer to and farther from the lamb as needed for even cooking, adding more hardwood to the fire when necessary. (It is easier to move the fire than to move the lamb.) Cook the lamb, basting it every 20 to 30 minutes with the brine and rosemary brush, until golden in places, about 3 hours.

Put on the fireplace gloves (the rebar will be very hot). Turn the lamb 180 degrees and lean it towards the fire to cook the other side. Cook, basting every 20 to 30 minutes with the brine and rosemary brush, until the lamb is medium, another 2½ to 3½ hours. Carefully remove the lamb from the fire. Let the lamb rest 30 minutes.

Bring the remaining brine to a boil then keep warm over low heat. Carve the lamb and serve, brushed with some of the brine.

ROAST LAMB SANDWICHES
with Tahini and Pickled Onions

We use slices of our Seven Fires–Style Roast Lamb (page 118) for these sandwiches, but the Sear-Crusted Leg of Lamb (page 114) also works nicely. Either way, this take on a classic gyro is a fantastic alternative to a burger.

SERVES 6 TO 8

2 cups baby kale

8 flatbreads or large pitas, warmed

½ lemon

1¾ pounds roast lamb, thinly sliced

Fine sea salt

½ cup organic tahini

Water, as needed

½ cup Pickled Red Onions (page 225)

Scatter the kale over the flatbreads, then squeeze the lemon over the kale. Divide the lamb between the sandwiches, then sprinkle with salt to taste. Whisk together the tahini with some water to thin it, and drizzle over the lamb. Scatter the pickled onions over the sandwiches and serve.

THE BUTCHER BLOCK

Both lamb and goat have rich flavor yet are low in fat, easy to raise, and a cinch to butcher. Seam cutting a lamb or a goat is akin to taking apart a jigsaw puzzle—the pieces just separate naturally. We often get requests for Frenched lamb chops, and while we will French the rack, it always feels like such a waste. That fat turns into a sizzling, crisp layer when broiled or grilled—think lamb bacon. When it comes to whole legs, there is always some debate over whether or not to remove the bone. Bones add flavor to the meat as it cooks, but can be cumbersome, too. Luckily, we have recipes for both approaches, each with great results. —*Alexi*

SEARED LAMB KIDNEYS
with Eggs and Cippolini Agrodolce

An overnight soak in milk and salt draws out the typical ammoniated note associated with kidneys and leaves us with a finely nuanced piece of meat, the centerpiece of this hearty salad course. Ask your butcher to leave the fat on the kidneys for extra flavor.

SERVES 4

1 quart whole milk

Fine sea salt

4 (3-ounce) lamb kidneys, still encased in their fat

4 large eggs

2 cups frisée lettuce

½ cup Cippolini Agrodolce (page 222)

2 tablespoons Pickled Mustard Seeds (page 212)

Whisk together the milk and 1 tablespoon salt in a medium bowl. Add the kidneys to the milk mixture and soak, refrigerated, for 24 hours.

Place the eggs in a medium saucepan and cover with tepid water. Bring the water to a boil, then turn off the heat and cover the saucepan, letting the eggs stand in the hot water for 6 minutes. Transfer the eggs to a bowl of very cold water to cool, then peel.

Drain the kidneys and pat dry. Score the fat halfway through, taking care not to cut into the kidneys themselves.

Heat a dry heavy skillet over high heat until very hot. Sear the kidneys, turning occasionally, until well browned and an instant-read thermometer registers 115°F. Transfer the kidneys to a cutting board and let rest for 10 minutes.

Divide the frisée among 4 plates. Slice the kidneys and divide among the plates. Top each salad with an egg and some of the cippolini agrodolce and pickled mustard seeds.

MARKET

As dusk falls, the restaurant at Wyebrook Farm glows like a stone lantern as laughter and conversation float out over the now empty fields.

GOAT IN HAY

Out here in farmland, we've got plenty of hay to go around, and it imparts a distinctly grassy flavor to this roast. If you don't have that same kind of access, you can find organic hay at an equine supply store. Serve the goat with a side of Chunky Potatoes (page 128) and an array of piquant condiments, such as Plum Mustard Relish (page 218) and Roasted Tomato and Mustard Relish (page 217).

SERVES 8 TO 10

1 (5- to 5½-pound) bone-in hind leg of goat

Fine sea salt

An armful of fresh, clean hay

2½ pounds small onions, unpeeled and halved

3 heads garlic, cloves separated

If necessary, find the tendon at the bottom of the leg (it is to the rear of the lowest joint), and sever it with a sharp knife (this helps the meat cook more evenly). Truss the leg at 2-inch intervals with kitchen string. Rub the leg all over with 1½ teaspoons salt and place in a roasting pan. Refrigerate the goat leg, uncovered, overnight.

Preheat the oven to 350°F. Soak the hay in warm water for 10 minutes.

Line the bottom of a roasting pan with ⅓ of the hay, taking care to lay pieces of hay in the same direction. Place a second layer of hay crosswise across the pan, so that it drapes over the edges of the pan. Arrange the onions and garlic cloves in an even layer on the hay then place the goat leg over top. Bring the overhanging hay up and over the goat leg, tucking in the ends, then place the remaining hay over the goat, in the same direction as the bottom layer and tuck the hay down and around the goat leg; it should be completely covered in hay. Transfer to the oven and roast until the meat is very tender and falling apart, 4½ to 5 hours.

Preheat the grill, preferably with hardwood or hardwood charcoal. Transfer the goat to a cutting board and loosely cover with foil (or hay) to keep warm.

(recipe continues)

Remove the roasted garlic cloves and onions from the hay. Peel the garlic cloves and set aside. Grill the onions until charred in places, then peel and coarsely chop them.

Pull the goat off the bone in large chunks and transfer to a serving platter. Scatter the roasted garlic and grilled onions over the goat and serve.

CHUNKY POTATOES

These are some of our favorite spuds. We shake parboiled potatoes vigorously in a pot with some fat to break up their outsides then roast them in a blistering oven for a crisp crust and buttery inside.

SERVES 8 TO 10

10 medium Yukon Gold potatoes (about 5 pounds), peeled and halved (quartered if large)

½ cup melted rendered animal fat or olive oil

Fine sea salt

Preheat the oven to 450°F. Boil the potatoes in a large pot of well-salted water until just cooked through, 20 to 25 minutes. Drain the potatoes and return them to the pot. Shake the pot back and forth to rough up the potatoes. Add the fat to the pot and shake the pot to coat the potatoes with the fat. Transfer the potatoes to a roasting pan. Roast the potatoes until crisp and browned, about 30 minutes. Season to taste with salt and serve immediately.

SPRING PICKLE AND BITTER GREEN SALAD *with Pickling Liquid Gastrique*

Flavor is all around us, even when we don't realize it. Reducing pickling liquid might seem like an extreme step in a vinaigrette technique, but the result is so beguiling that you'll never look at your pantry pickles the same way again.

SERVES 4

½ cup chopped Spring Pickles (page 227), plus ½ cup pickling liquid

¼ cup extra-virgin olive oil

Fine sea salt and freshly ground black pepper

3 tablespoons rendered animal fat or extra-virgin olive oil

1 cup fresh bread cubes

8 cups mixed bitter greens, such as radicchio, watercress, frisée, and arugula

Boil the pickling liquid in a small heavy saucepan until it is reduced to 2 tablespoons. Remove from the heat and let cool slightly, then whisk in the oil. Season the dressing with salt and pepper to taste. Set aside.

Heat the rendered fat in a large heavy skillet over medium heat until hot, then add the bread cubes and toast, stirring frequently, until crisp and golden, about 8 minutes. Remove from the heat.

Put the bitter greens and the chopped pickles in a large salad bowl and toss gently with the dressing to coat. Divide the salad among serving plates. Garnish with the croutons and serve.

GOAT, TOMATO, AND GREEN CORIANDER RAGU *with Pici Pasta*

If you have yet to introduce goat meat to your kitchen, start here and don't look back. This makes a large batch of ragu (about 3½ quarts), which is more than you'll need for a meal. Don't fret—it freezes very nicely.

SERVES 6 TO 8

1 (6- to 7-pound) bone-in goat shoulder

Fine sea salt and freshly ground black pepper

2 tablespoons extra-virgin olive oil

8 cups Roasted Tomato Purée (page 230)

2 onions, chopped

2 garlic cloves, finely chopped

½ cup crushed Dehydrated Sweet Peppers (page 239)

2 tablespoons Dried Green Coriander (page 238)

Pici Pasta (page 211)

¼ cup fresh cilantro leaves

Preheat a grill with hardwood or hardwood charcoal. Preheat the oven to 350°F.

Cut the goat into pieces at the joints, or have a butcher do this for you. When the fire burns down to charcoal, season the goat all over with 1½ teaspoons salt and grill, turning occasionally, until browned, about 12 minutes. Remove from the heat.

Brush the goat with the oil, then transfer to a deep baking dish, along with the tomato purée, onions, garlic, dehydrated sweet peppers, and coriander. Cover the dish tightly with aluminum foil, then braise in the oven until the meat is very tender and falling off the bone, about 3½ hours. Let the meat cool in the sauce until warm (or overnight).

Remove the goat from the sauce and shred the meat, discarding the bones. Transfer the shredded meat to a saucepan, along with the sauce. Bring the sauce to a simmer on the stove top. Season the sauce with salt and pepper to taste.

Cook the pasta in a large pot of boiling salted water until al dente, about 6 minutes. Drain well then toss with enough of the sauce to coat. Serve sprinkled with the fresh cilantro leaves.

GOAT'S MILK DULCE DE LECHE

Dulce de leche's complex caramelized flavor is the result of a surprisingly straightforward process. It does, however, require vigilance when stirring, especially in the last half hour of cooking when the bottom of the pot is prone to scorching. Goat's milk is a classic Mexican choice for this sauce and adds just the right amount of barnyard funk to the sweet mix.

MAKES ABOUT 2⅔ CUPS

8 cups goat's milk

2 cups sugar

1 teaspoon vanilla

½ teaspoon baking soda

1 tablespoon water

Combine the goat's milk, sugar, and vanilla in a large heavy pot and bring to a boil. Remove from the heat. Stir together the baking soda and water in a small bowl and add to the milk mixture, letting the mixture foam and subside. Return the pot to the heat and boil, stirring frequently and taking care it does not boil over, until the mixture is thickened and pale golden, about 1 hour. Continue cooking, stirring frequently so the mixture does not stick to the bottom of the pot, until it is golden caramel colored and thickened, 35 to 45 minutes more.

Pour the dulce de leche through a fine-mesh sieve into a bowl or jar. If not using right away, let the dulce de leche cool completely then cover tightly and store in the refrigerator for up to 1 month.

BLUEBERRY-DULCE DE LECHE GRATINS

This summery fruit gratin might seem too simple to be true, but something transformative happens after just a few minutes under the broiler. While the hickory nuts toast and crisp, the berries soften and burst, releasing their sweet-tart juice, which then mingles with the melting dulce de leche. The resulting dish is balanced and nuanced—a perfect base for a scoop of ice cream.

SERVES 8

3 cups fresh blueberries

1 cup Goat's Milk Dulce de Leche (page 133)

¼ cup chopped hickory nuts or hazelnuts

Vanilla ice cream, for serving

Preheat the broiler. Divide the blueberries among 8 shallow flame-proof gratin dishes. Drizzle the dulce de leche over the blueberries, then scatter the hickory nuts over top.

Broil the gratins about 5 inches from the heat until the blueberries have just started to burst, and the dulce de leche is melted, about 2 minutes. Serve the gratins warm with vanilla ice cream.

CHICKEN

Healthier, Tastier Birds

If you've ever thought about raising your own chickens and have looked into which breeds might be best for you, you've probably felt overwhelmed. There are layers with their rainbow-colored eggs, broilers that grow fast, those that grow slowly, and mixed breeds that are supposed to be good at everything. Deciding what birds to raise at Wyebrook comes down to a mixture of philosophy and practicality.

In the industrial system, it is easier to sell a chicken with more breast meat to a grocery store, and the faster that bird can grow, the more profitable it is. The modern industrial chicken, the Cornish Cross, is ready for slaughter in about 40 days. That's just over 5 weeks. Every time I think about that time frame, I am shocked. There is a huge downside to this efficiency, mostly for the chicken. The bird's musculature grows at an incredible speed, much faster than its skeletal and circulatory system. As it matures, a Cornish Cross can barely move and is susceptible to heart attacks. To me, that kind of genetic selection is nothing more than animal cruelty.

At the other end of the spectrum, you find the true heritage breeds. These birds are much closer genetically to their ancestors, but take longer to finish, sometimes 20 to 30 weeks. I would love to use these birds, but we have not been able to find a way to raise them at an economical price. And I'm not sure I can say this too many times: An enormous factor in sustainable farming is the financial sustainability of the farm.

Our broiler chickens, which go by various names—K-22, Freedom Rangers—depending on the hatchery, are brown birds that take nine to 10 weeks to finish. These birds are extremely active foragers, making them well suited for Wyebrook's pastures where they graze on grass and insects. (This is also why we only raise broilers in the spring, summer, and fall.) The exercise they get makes for meat with a denser texture and a deeper, more, well, chicken-y flavor than a bird raised in a confinement house. Their eggs are generous, with deep-orange yolks. We supplement their diet with a small amount of grain, but they get a significant portion of their nutrients from what they find. The result is a happy hen with delicious yellow fat full of Omega 3s. —*Dean*

SUPER-CRUST SPATCHCOCKED CHICKEN

This technique is the same that we use for our Sear-Crusted Leg of Lamb (page 114). The unhurried browning followed by time in a low oven leads to crisp, flavorful skin and wonderfully juicy meat. At the height of summer, this bird is glorious with a dead-ripe tomato salad. In winter, we like to pair this with a batch of Sauerkraut (page 224) and golden squares of Pommes Anna.

SERVES 4 TO 6

1 (3- to 4-pound) chicken

Fine sea salt

Remove the backbone of the chicken with kitchen shears by cutting along either side of the spine (reserve for stock). Remove the keel bone (see page 149). Tuck the wings behind the breasts, then tuck the legs in so that the bottoms of the drumsticks are pointed away from the body and the chicken is as flat as possible. Sprinkle the chicken evenly with 1 teaspoon salt.

Preheat the oven to 225°F. Heat a large dry heavy skillet over high heat until hot (a 3-pound bird will fit into a 12-inch skillet; anything bigger will need a 14-inch or larger skillet). Place the chicken in the skillet, skin side down, and immediately lower the heat to medium low. Sear the chicken without moving, until the skin is dark golden brown, about 15 minutes. Flip the chicken over and transfer the skillet to the oven. Roast the chicken until just cooked through, about 30 minutes. Transfer the chicken to a cutting board and let stand for 10 to 15 minutes. Carve the chicken into serving pieces.

POMMES ANNA

If you want to serve this with the Super-Crust Spatchcocked Chicken, brown the squares of potatoes in the fat remaining in the skillet from cooking the bird. Otherwise, use the rendered fat or olive oil called for below.

SERVES 8

3 pounds russet potatoes

½ cup (1 stick) unsalted butter, melted

Fine sea salt and freshly ground black pepper

¼ cup rendered animal fat or olive oil

Preheat the oven to 350°F. Peel the potatoes and slice very thinly using an adjustable-blade slicer. Butter a 9-inch square baking pan. Layer the potatoes evenly in the pan, sprinkling each layer with a generous pinch each of salt and pepper and drizzling each layer with some of the melted butter. Drizzle the remaining butter evenly over the top layer of potatoes and press down on the potatoes to force them into the pan. Cover the pan with aluminum foil and bake until the potatoes are very tender, about 1½ hours.

Oil the bottom of a second 9-inch pan. Remove the aluminum foil from the potatoes and place the oiled pan on top of the potatoes. Place a weight (such as cans of tomatoes) on top of the upper pan and refrigerate until the potatoes are cold.

When ready to serve, trim off the outer ½-inch from the potatoes. Cut the remaining 8-inch square of potatoes into 16 (2 x 2-inch) pieces. Heat the rendered fat in a large skillet over high heat until hot. Working in batches if necessary, place the potato squares in the skillet and sear, turning once, until golden brown and crisp on the outsides and hot in the center, about 10 minutes total. Serve immediately.

CHICKEN BALLOTINE

A chicken, stripped of its bones, gets reformed into a log and re-wrapped in its own skin. It's a classic French technique that actually feels very modern. Once the ballotine is cooked through at a moderate temperature, we crank up the oven until the skin becomes burnished and crisp to the point of crackling. We serve this with Farro Risotto with Morels and Asparagus (page 145) on cool spring nights or with Lemony Celery Salad (page 144) year-round.

SERVES 6

1 (3½-pound) chicken

¼ cup heavy cream

¼ cup finely grated Parmigiano Reggiano

1 garlic clove

3 ice cubes

Fine sea salt and freshly ground black pepper

Preheat the oven to 300°F. Place the chicken on a work surface. Feel for the wing joints that connect to the breasts. Cut through the joints, disconnecting the wings from the chicken. Reserve the wings for stock.

Place the chicken breast side down, then cut through the skin from the neck to the tail. Working on the left side, gently work your fingers under the skin to loosen it from the carcass. Work the skin away from the meat, pulling the legs out from under their skins, taking care not to tear the skin. Reserve the skin.

Remove the legs from the carcass, then remove the meat from the leg bones and reserve the meat. Remove the breast meat from the carcass, reserving the meat. Reserve the bones for making stock.

Remove the tenders from the breasts, then cut away and discard the tendons from the tenders. Cut the tenders and the leg meat into ½-inch cubes. Pulse the tenders with the cream, Parmigiano Reggiano, garlic clove, ice cubes, ½ teaspoon salt, and ¼ teaspoon pepper in a food processor until finely chopped. Add the leg meat and pulse until the leg meat is coarsely chopped and combined. Cut the breasts lengthwise into ½-inch-wide strips.

(recipe continues)

Gently spread the skin out on a work surface, with the long side nearest you. Trim it into a 16 x 8-inch rectangle by cutting through the wing holes to make one long side. Trim some of the excess skin to patch the other long side of the rectangle. Spread half of the ground filling lengthwise down the center of the skin. Place the strips of breasts, overlapping in a cross-hatch pattern, over the ground meat. Season the strips with salt. Spread the remaining ground meat over the layer of strips.

Fold half the skin up and over the filling, then fold the other half of skin over the filling, enclosing it like a letter. Place a large sheet of aluminum foil on a work surface, with a long side nearest you. Tightly roll the ballotine up in the foil to make a long cylinder, crimping the ends as you roll. Place the ballotine in a roasting pan and bake until cooked through, about 1 hour. Let the ballotine rest in the foil at room temperature for 30 minutes. Increase the oven temperature to 450°F.

Open the foil, forming it into a cupped trough that will hold the ballotine and any accumulated juices. Return the ballotine, in the foil trough, to the oven and roast, rotating the ballotine in the foil package as it browns, until it is browned all over, about 30 minutes. (The juices in the foil will baste the ballotine as it is rotated.)

To serve, slice the ballotine into 1-inch-thick pieces and serve drizzled with some of the accumulated juices.

LEMONY CELERY SALAD

This simple salad comes together in minutes and adds bright flavor and crisp texture to any meal.

SERVES 6

1 large head celery

3 tablespoons extra-virgin olive oil

1 teaspoon freshly grated lemon zest

2 tablespoons lemon juice

Fine sea salt and freshly ground black pepper

Separate and trim the celery ribs. Reserve any inner leaves. Slice the ribs crosswise, then toss the celery with the oil, lemon zest, juice, the reserved celery leaves, and ¼ teaspoon each salt and pepper.

FARRO RISOTTO WITH MORELS AND ASPARAGUS

The pop and chew of farro, an ancient grain, offers plenty of interest to this risotto. If you can't find dried mushrooms, you can substitute a pound of sliced fresh crimini to produce a fast and surprisingly intense mushroom flavor.

SERVES 6

4 ounces dried mushrooms, such as shiitake, porcini, or morels

2 carrots

2 celery ribs

2 shallots, halved

6 parsley sprigs

1 bay leaf

1 teaspoon black peppercorns

10 cups water

2 cups farro

Fine sea salt and freshly ground black pepper

1 tablespoon rendered animal fat or unsalted butter

1 cup fresh morel mushrooms, halved if large

½ pound asparagus, trimmed and thinly sliced diagonally

1 cup Rich Chicken Stock (page 246)

1 tablespoon cornstarch

4 tablespoons unsalted butter

Wrap the dried mushrooms, carrots, celery, shallots, parsley, bay leaf, and peppercorns in a square of cheesecloth and tie into a bouquet garni with kitchen string. Put the bouquet garni into a medium heavy pot along with the water, farro, and ½ teaspoon salt. Bring to a boil then reduce the heat, and simmer, covered, until the farro is tender, about 45 minutes.

While the farro cooks, heat the rendered fat in a large heavy skillet over medium-high heat until hot. Add the morels and asparagus and cook, stirring occasionally, until golden in places, 6 to 8 minutes. Remove from the heat and set aside.

Remove the bouquet garni from the farro, pressing on the solids to extract as much liquid as possible. Stir the chicken stock and cornstarch together then add to the farro along with the butter and simmer, stirring, until slightly thickened, about 4 minutes. Stir in the morels and asparagus, season with salt to taste, then serve.

A litter of Tamworth piglets spends its first few weeks in the safety of a pen, but soon they, like the chickens, will be free to roam and forage.

CHICKEN BOUDIN BLANC

Similar to the fine white veal sausages you might find in France or Germany, this version is made with chicken and warmly spiced.

MAKES ABOUT 3 POUNDS

5 tablespoons unsalted butter

1½ cups chopped sweet onion

1 teaspoon fresh thyme leaves

¾ teaspoon finely ground mixed black and white peppercorns

¼ teaspoon ground cinnamon

¼ teaspoon ground allspice

¼ teaspoon freshly grated nutmeg

2 pounds boneless skinless chicken meat, preferably a combination of dark and white meat, coarsely chopped

7 ounces pork fatback

Fine sea salt

½ cup fresh breadcrumbs

¼ cup heavy cream

About 5 feet of hog casings

EQUIPMENT: **Sausage stuffer, a pin**

Heat 3 tablespoons butter in a small heavy saucepan over medium heat, add the onions and cook, stirring occasionally, until translucent, about 7 minutes. Stir in the thyme, pepper, cinnamon, allspice, and nutmeg, and cook, stirring occasionally, until very fragrant, about 2 minutes. Remove from the heat and cool completely.

Toss the chicken and fatback together with 1½ teaspoons salt, then grind using a ⅛-inch die on a meat grinder and let it fall into a chilled bowl set over ice.

Put the breadcrumbs and cream in a food processor and pulse to combine. Add the meats and chilled onion mixture then pulse until smooth.

Using a sausage stuffer, fill the casings with the filling, twisting the casings to make 6- to 8-inch links. Prick each link with the pin. Chill the sausages overnight.

Bring a large pot of water to 180°F. Gently poach the sausages until cooked through, about 10 minutes. Chill the sausages until ready to serve.

To serve, heat the remaining 2 tablespoons butter in a large heavy skillet over medium-high heat until hot. Sear the boudin blanc, turning occasionally, until browned and heated through, about 6 minutes total.

THE BUTCHER BLOCK

Chicken is the most accessible animal to butcher, due to its manageable size and the very fact that it is so easy to get one whole. The chicken practically comes with its own instruction manual in the form of fat lines that run over the joints, like the one that connects the drumstick and thigh. To find it, place the whole leg, skin side down, on the work surface. You'll see the line of fat running crosswise across the leg. Place your knife on the edge of that line, to the side of the drumstick, and slice downward. You'll go right through the joint every time. Look for other lines along the underside of the breasts—cut through them to remove the ribs and spine, and you'll be left with the bone-in breasts. Couldn't be simpler.

Perhaps the greatest way to butcher a chicken is spatchcocking. To do so, remove the backbone—a knife works, but kitchen shears make easier work of it—then tear out the keel bone. To do this, place the chicken, breast side down, on the work surface and make an incision with your knife through the top of the breast bone, cutting through cartilage until you hit the bone (don't cut through it). Put down your knife and run your thumbs down and around the keel bone—the bottom of which is cartilage—then pull it out by hand. This allows you to make the chicken as flat as possible, which means it will cook quickly and evenly for a super moist bird. —*Alexi*

CHICKEN RAVIOLI IN BRODO

Poaching the chicken in our rich chicken stock and then simmering the ravioli in that now double-rich stock packs this delicate soup with intense chicken flavor. If you're not making your own ricotta you can substitute store-bought.

SERVES 12

4 quarts Rich Chicken Stock (page 246)

Fine sea salt and freshly ground pepper

1 (3- to 3½-pound) chicken

3 cups baby spinach

2 cups Fresh Ricotta (page 240)

1 cup finely grated Parmigiano Reggiano

½ teaspoon ground mace

Fresh Pasta Dough, rolled out for ravioli into 8 sheets (page 207)

Parmesan Chips (page 154), for serving

2 tablespoons chopped flat-leaf parsley (optional), for serving

Bring the stock to a simmer in a large pot, and season with salt to taste. Place the chicken in the stock, breast side down, cover, and simmer for 25 minutes. Remove the pot from the heat, turn the chicken over, and let stand, covered, for 15 minutes more. Uncover the pot and let the chicken rest in the stock, chilled, overnight.

Transfer the chicken to a work surface. Remove the meat and skin, discarding the bones. Working in batches, combine the chicken meat and skin, spinach, ricotta, Parmigiano Reggiano, mace, 1 teaspoon salt, and ½ teaspoon pepper in a food processor and pulse until finely chopped.

Place 1 sheet of pasta on a cleaned, dry work surface. Place 2 teaspoons of the chicken filling at 2-inch intervals along the pasta sheet. Lightly brush water around each mound of filling with a pastry brush, then drape another sheet of pasta over the first sheet, pressing the pasta together around the filling to remove any air bubbles.

(recipe continues)

Cut the ravioli from the pasta sheets with a 3¼-inch round cutter. Repeat with the remaining pasta sheets and filling to make about 48 ravioli. Save any leftover filling for another use.

Bring the stock back to a gentle boil then drop the ravioli into the stock and cook until al dente, 5 to 6 minutes. Serve the ravioli and stock in bowls (reserve the leftover broth for another use), garnished with the Parmesan chips and parsley, if you like.

PARMESAN CHIPS

Parmesan chips are a must in every cook's arsenal. They're easy to make and become an impressive garnish for soups and salads, but they offer a temptation for the cook, too. Try just one and you'll have trouble getting them out of the kitchen.

MAKES ABOUT 15

½ cup finely grated Parmigiano Reggiano

1 teaspoon all-purpose flour

Preheat the oven to 350°F. Line a baking sheet with a nonstick silicone liner or parchment paper.

Stir together the Parmigiano Reggiano and flour. Make teaspoon-sized mounds of the cheese mixture on the liner, leaving about 2 inches between each mound.

Bake the chips until pale golden, about 10 minutes. Cool on the baking sheet for 2 minutes, then transfer to a rack to cool completely.

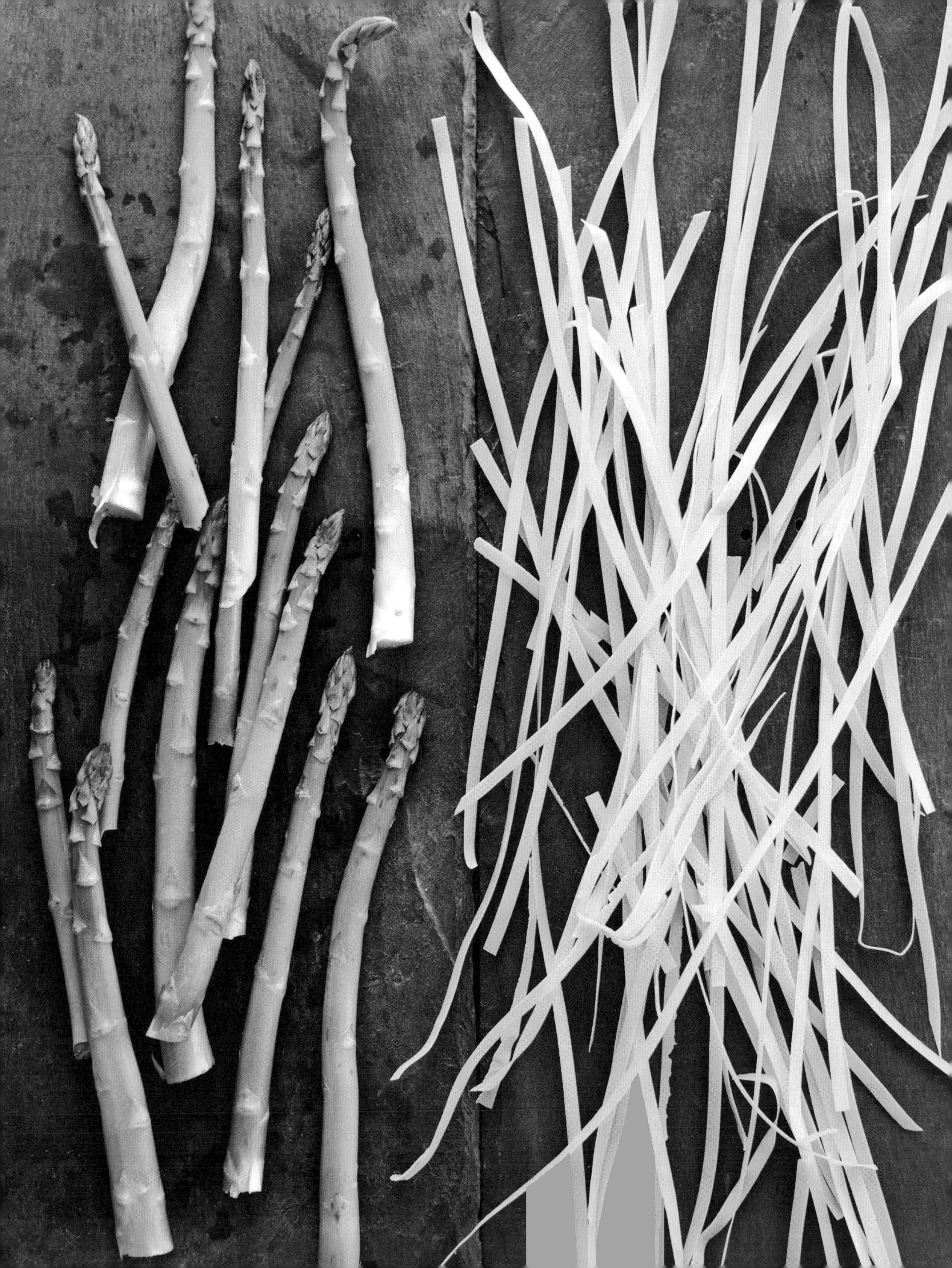

CONFIT GARLIC ALFREDO
with Poached Eggs and Asparagus

Buttery soft cloves of garlic are mashed into creamy Alfredo sauce, bringing a can't-put-your-finger-on-it sweetness to a tangle of fresh fettuccine.

SERVES 4 TO 6

2 tablespoons white distilled vinegar

4 large eggs

8 ounces fresh Fettuccine (page 207)

2 tablespoons extra-virgin olive oil

1 pound asparagus, trimmed and thinly sliced on the diagonal

Fine sea salt and freshly ground black pepper

4 cloves Garlic Confit (page 243), peeled

1 cup heavy cream

½ cup finely grated Valley Shepherd Pepato cheese or Parmigiano Reggiano

Fill a large deep skillet halfway with water and stir in the vinegar. Bring the liquid to a bare simmer. Break each egg into a measuring cup and then slide it into the barely simmering water, adding them in a circle so you can take them out in the same order. Simmer the eggs for about 1½ minutes (for runny yolks). Using a slotted spoon, transfer the eggs to a bowl of warm water to reserve.

Cook the fettuccine in boiling salted water until al dente. Reserve 1½ cups of the pasta cooking water, then drain the pasta.

Heat the oil in a large heavy skillet over medium-high heat until hot. Add the asparagus, ½ teaspoon salt, and ¼ teaspoon pepper and cook, stirring frequently, until the asparagus is golden, 3 to 4 minutes. Add the garlic, mashing the cloves with a spoon so they melt. Stir in ¾ cup of the reserved pasta cooking water and bring to a boil. Stir in the cream and boil until the sauce is the desired thickness, 2 to 3 minutes.

Add the pasta, tossing gently to coat with the sauce. Thin with additional pasta cooking water, if desired, then season with salt and pepper to taste.

To serve, divide the pasta among serving plates. Top each plate with a poached egg and sprinkle with the cheese.

Butter Lettuce Salad with Ash-Cooked Eggs

BUTTER LETTUCE SALAD
with Ash-Cooked Eggs

Baking eggs in the ashes of a wood fire can take a little practice—if the ashes are still too hot, the eggs may explode (exciting, but not very helpful). It's best to spread the ashes of the fire thinly over the bottom of the grill so you can see where there may still be embers, then nestle the eggs in an ember-free area and mound ashes around them. If you get the temperature right, the eggs will be perfectly cooked in about 15 minutes.

SERVES 4

1 head butter lettuce

⅓ cup crumbled blue cheese, such as Bertrand Blue

¼ cup buttermilk

¼ cup mayonnaise

2 tablespoons sour cream

1 teaspoon finely grated lemon zest

2 teaspoons lemon juice

¼ cup finely chopped mixed fresh, tender herbs, such as basil, tarragon, dill, parsley, and chives

Fine sea salt and freshly ground black pepper

4 large ash-cooked or hard-boiled eggs, peeled and sliced

Tear the lettuce into large pieces and place on a serving platter. Scatter the cheese over the lettuce.

Whisk together the buttermilk, mayonnaise, sour cream, lemon zest, lemon juice, herbs, ½ teaspoon salt, and ¼ teaspoon pepper. Drizzle the dressing over the lettuce. Arrange the eggs over the salad, sprinkle with salt, and serve.

CANDIED ORANGE PAVLOVA

Pavlova, a meringue that is at once shatteringly crisp and marshmallow-y soft, is a blank canvas of a dessert and a fine way to use up any egg whites left over from making fresh pasta.

SERVES 6 TO 8

1¼ cups plus 2 teaspoons superfine sugar

2 teaspoons cornstarch

4 large egg whites, at room temperature

Fine sea salt

2 teaspoons lemon juice or white distilled vinegar

½ teaspoon vanilla extract

1¼ cups heavy cream

1 tablespoon orange liqueur, such as Grand Marnier

¾ cup whole Candied Valencia Orange slices with some syrup (page 237) or fresh berries

Preheat the oven to 275°F. Line a baking sheet with a sheet of parchment paper. Stir together 2 teaspoons of the sugar with the cornstarch and reserve.

Beat the egg whites with ¼ teaspoon salt in the large bowl of an electric mixer until soft peaks form, about 2 minutes. With the mixer running, add the remaining 1¼ cups sugar, 1 tablespoon at a time. Beat in the cornstarch mixture, then add the lemon juice and vanilla. Continue beating until stiff glossy peaks form, another 1 to 2 minutes.

Pile the meringue onto the parchment and, using an offset spatula or the back of a spoon, spread it into an 8-inch round, about 2½ inches high around the edge and slightly lower in the center, to make a nest.

Place the meringue in the oven and reduce the heat to 250°F. Bake the meringue until crisp, dry, and slightly colored, about 45 minutes. Rotate the baking sheet and continue baking until hard on the outside and slightly darker, 45 minutes more. Turn off the heat and leave the meringue in the oven to dry for at least 30 minutes. Gently peel off the parchment, and transfer the meringue to a platter.

Beat the cream and orange liqueur together until soft peaks form, then fill the center of the meringue with the cream. Top the pavlova with the candied oranges or fresh berries.

GOAT CHEESE SEMIFREDDO

with Raspberries in Lemon Verbena Syrup

Goat cheese adds a subtly savory, tangy note to the classic Italian frozen mousse. It plays very well with raspberries or wineberries, brilliant little fruits that we forage from local hedgerows when they ripen in mid-July.

SERVES 6 TO 8

FOR THE SEMIFREDDO

2 cups heavy cream

¾ cup sugar

Fine sea salt

2 tablespoons cornstarch

2 tablespoons cold water

¼ cup crumbled fresh goat cheese

4 large egg whites

FOR THE WINEBERRIES IN LEMON VERBENA SYRUP

1 cup sugar

1 cup dry white wine

4 sprigs fresh or dried lemon verbena

2 cups fresh raspberries or wineberries, if available

Fine sea salt

EQUIPMENT: **A (5-cup) terrine mold**

Make the semifreddo: Whisk together 1 cup of the cream, the sugar, and ⅛ teaspoon salt in a small saucepan. Stir together the cornstarch and water, then combine with the cream mixture. Place the saucepan over medium-high heat and cook, stirring frequently, until the mixture comes to a boil and thickens, 1 to 2 minutes. Remove the saucepan from the heat and whisk in the goat cheese to combine. Chill the goat cheese mixture until cold.

Beat the remaining 1 cup cream until it holds soft peaks. Fold the cream into the goat cheese mixture. Beat the egg whites with ⅛ teaspoon salt until they hold soft peaks. Fold the egg whites into the goat cheese mixture, then pour into the loaf pan and freeze completely, about 5 hours.

While the semifreddo freezes, make the lemon verbena syrup: Combine the sugar, wine, and lemon verbena in a small heavy saucepan and bring to a boil, then remove from the heat and let the syrup steep, covered, for 10 minutes. Place the berries in a bowl, then pour the syrup through a fine-mesh sieve over the berries. Let the berries cool to room temperature.

To serve, fill a roasting pan with warm water. Set the terrine in the warm water for 30 seconds, then run a knife around the edge and invert the semifreddo onto a serving platter. Cut the semifreddo into thick slices. Serve the semifreddo with the berries and syrup spooned over top.

A NEW YEAR'S EVE FARM MENU

Long since closed, the Shartlesville Inn was a stone farmhouse along old Route 22 where Amish or Mennonite women made big batches of toasted sweet corn pudding and crisp scrapple. They served everything family-style to guests sitting at communal tables. It was simple food in a simple setting. We passed dishes around the table to strangers and soon, they were strangers no longer.

With its shared tables and regional food, Wyebrook could be a modern version of the Shartlesville Inn. I saw this for myself when Dean asked me to cook New Year's Eve dinner. On a holiday normally reserved for insular couples, that sense of togetherness was amplified, and Dean refused to ramp up the prices or turn the tables. When you sit down at the Wyebrook table for a New Year's Eve feast, you're in it for the night.

When we started planning the menu, Dean had suggested duck. His had been living on the pond and were ready to be butchered. My creative juices started flowing. But I got a call a few days later—no ducks. No one could catch them. Dean had even bribed his nephews $5 a bird, but the ducks were too wily. So I changed menu direction (and the ducks still call the pond home).

The pasta course ended up being an alicot with handmade gnocchi. Traditionally, alicot is a peasant-style ragu made from chicken giblets, stewed together with wine and stock. Inspired by the delicious Devons that Dean raises, I experimented with an all-beef alicot. We grilled beef cheeks, heart, tongue, and liver over a hardwood fire then leisurely stewed the meats together for 12 hours. The liver was puréed and added back to the sauce to become the richest, deepest ragu you can imagine.

No one left the New Year's dinner hungry. The guests stayed, talking and laughing late into the night. But they left eventually. And then, there I was, in the barnyard alone with the stars. Stars alone are a wonder to gaze at, but when they become part of a constellation, their story means much more. That happened at dinner. People came as couples or singles and became, even if only for a few hours, something bigger: A constellation brought together by food, welcoming in a brand new year. —*Ian*

SMOKED CHILE PORK SCHMALTZ

The fat that cooks out of the Smoked Chile–Braised Pork Belly (page 177) is too spicy to be used for cooking fat, but makes a complex compound "butter" when whipped with red onion, parsley, and lemon. At our New Year's Eve dinner, we served this spread with loaves of Buttermilk Sourdough Pan d'Epi (page 203).

MAKES ABOUT 2 CUPS

1½ cups rendered pork fat, reserved from making Smoked Chile–Braised Pork Belly (page 177)

3 tablespoons finely chopped red onion

3 tablespoons finely chopped flat-leaf parsley

2 teaspoons finely grated lemon zest

1 tablespoon lemon juice

Fine sea salt and freshly ground black pepper

Crusty bread, for serving

Using an electric mixer fitted with a whisk attachment, whip together the pork fat, onion, parsley, lemon zest, and juice until fluffy. Season the schmaltz with salt and pepper to taste. Serve with crusty bread.

DIRT-FED BEETS, MANY WAYS

This dish is crafted from several individual recipes, each of which is wonderful all on its own. Both kinds of pickled beets are great additions to salads, the beet chips are fine snacking all by themselves, and the beet purée pairs well with just about any roasted meat. But when these parts are combined on one plate the dish becomes a most whimsical take on the classic beet and blue cheese salad. To assemble the dish, spoon some beet purée on a plate and sprinkle a handful of beet dirt over it. Scatter the quick and slow pickled beets over the dirt. Finish with a drizzle of blue cheese yogurt and a few beet chips for garnish.

MAKES 10 FIRST COURSES

QUICK PICKLED GOLDEN BEETS

Turmeric boosts the golden hue of these quick pickles.

MAKES ABOUT 1 QUART

4 cups water

1 cup white wine vinegar

⅓ cup sugar

1 tablespoon ground turmeric

Fine sea salt

2 bunches medium golden beets, trimmed, peeled, and cut into ½-inch cubes

Combine the water, vinegar, sugar, turmeric, and 1 tablespoon salt in a medium saucepan and bring to a boil, stirring until the sugar is dissolved. Remove from the heat. Place the beets in the hot pickling liquid and let stand at room temperature for at least 2 hours. If making ahead, the beets keep, refrigerated in the pickling liquid, for up to 1 month.

PICKLED BULL'S BLOOD BEETS AND ONIONS

By roasting these beets before they are submerged in their pickling liquid, we've intensified their goodness. We favor the heirloom variety of beet called Bull's Blood, with its dark red leaves, but any red beets will do. Serve these with Blood Sausage (page 31) for a little blood on "blood" action or all by themselves as a simple snack or cocktail hors d'oeuvre.

MAKES ABOUT 6 PINTS

6 pounds small red beets, preferably Bull's Blood

Fine sea salt

2½ cups red wine vinegar

1¼ cups water

⅓ cup sugar

1 dried hot chile

1 bay leaf

½ teaspoon coriander seeds

½ teaspoon black peppercorns

2 small red onions, sliced into ¼-inch wedges

2 garlic cloves, smashed

Preheat the oven to 450°F. Trim the beets and divide between 2 large sheets of aluminum foil. Sprinkle with 1 tablespoon salt, then wrap tightly in foil. Roast the beets until tender, 1¼ to 1½ hours.

Let the beets cool slightly in the foil, then unwrap, and slip the skins from the beets. Halve the beets (or quarter if large).

Combine the vinegar, water, sugar, dried chile, bay leaf, coriander, peppercorns, and 2¼ teaspoons salt in a medium saucepan and bring to a simmer, stirring until the sugar and salt are dissolved. Remove from the heat and stir in the onions, garlic, and roasted beets. Let cool to room temperature. Transfer the beet mixture to an airtight container and store in the refrigerator for up to 1 month.

BEET PURÉE

Smear this blend on toasts and sprinkle with goat cheese for a fast hors d'oeuvre.

MAKES ABOUT 1½ CUPS

1 pound medium red beets

Fine sea salt

1 tablespoon apple cider vinegar

Preheat the oven to 400°F. Place the beets on a large sheet of aluminum foil. Sprinkle 1½ teaspoons salt over the beets and wrap tightly with the foil. Roast the beets until very tender, 1 to 1½ hours. Let the beets cool slightly, then slip off their skins and cut into chunks. Purée the beets in a blender with the vinegar until very smooth. Season to taste with salt. Serve the beet purée warm or chilled.

CANDY-STRIPED BEET CHIPS

These sweet chips keep for a month in a sealed container at room temperature.

MAKES ABOUT 60

4 medium Chioggia beets, trimmed and peeled

1 cup sugar

1 cup water

1 tablespoon white vinegar

Fine sea salt

Slice the beets into rounds, as thinly as possible. Combine the sugar, water, vinegar, and ½ teaspoon salt in a saucepan and bring to a boil, stirring until the sugar is dissolved. Remove from the heat. Place the beets in the hot syrup and let stand for 10 minutes.

Preheat the oven to 175°F. Line 2 baking sheets with parchment paper. Arrange slices in a single layer and bake until dry yet still slightly pliable, 30 to 40 minutes. Let 1 chip cool completely. If it becomes crisp, cool the rest of the chips. If still slightly pliable, continue to bake, checking at 5-minute intervals. If not using right away, transfer the chips to an airtight container.

BEET DIRT

A package of beets accidentally roasted all night and wasn't discovered until the next morning. Curiosity led us to cut one open: The core of the beet had turned into a deep, sticky caramel. Scooped out and blended with some breadcrumbs and dried mushrooms, the mixture looks and tastes like a deliciously sweet-sour nod to soil.

MAKES ABOUT 3 CUPS

2 pounds red beets

Fine sea salt and freshly ground black pepper

½ loaf week-old sourdough bread, cut into cubes

1 tablespoon dried porcini powder

Preheat the oven to 400°F. Place the beets on a large sheet of aluminum foil. Sprinkle 2 teaspoons salt over the beets then wrap tightly with the foil. Roast the beets until they are blackened and crisp, 10 hours or overnight. Let the beets cool slightly. Cut open the beets and scoop out the cores.

Put the bread in a food processor and pulse until it forms fine crumbs. Add the beet cores and porcini powder, and pulse to combine. Season with salt and pepper to taste.

BLUE CHEESE YOGURT

This tangy mix would be fantastic with chicken wings.

MAKES ABOUT 2 CUPS

1 cup buttermilk

4 ounces blue cheese

½ cup plain yogurt

Combine the buttermilk, blue cheese, and yogurt in a blender and purée until smooth. Place the mixture in a container with a lid and let stand at about 90°F overnight. Strain the yogurt through a fine-mesh sieve, discarding the drained liquid. Blue cheese yogurt keeps, refrigerated in an airtight container, for several weeks.

SMOKED CHILE-BRAISED PORK BELLY *with Turnip Purée*

Gently smoked peppers and chile, apple sweetness, and umami-packed miso all play together well in the pot, resulting in layers of flavor that penetrate the pork. The resulting reduced sauce is the picture of complexity, perfectly balanced.

SERVES 10

FOR THE PORK BELLY:

3 red bell peppers

1 fresh hot red chile

4 cups Rich Pork Stock (page 245) or Rich Beef Stock (page 248)

2 cups apple cider

¼ cup white miso

1 (3-pound) piece fresh pork belly

Fine sea salt and freshly ground black pepper

FOR THE TURNIP PURÉE:

2 pounds purple-top turnips, peeled and cut into chunks

Fine sea salt

½ cup (1 stick) unsalted butter

EQUIPMENT: **Hardwood smoker, hardwood chips, such as cherry, apple, or oak**

Make the pork belly: Preheat a hardwood smoker. Halve the peppers, discarding the seeds and cores. Smoke the peppers and chile, replenishing the smoker with hardwood chips as needed, for 3 hours. Transfer the peppers and chile to a blender and purée until smooth.

Preheat the oven to 350°F. Transfer the chile purée to a pot large enough to hold the pork belly. Add the stock, apple cider, and miso and whisk to combine. Season the pork belly with 1½ teaspoons salt and ½ teaspoon pepper, place in the braising liquid, and bring to a simmer on the stove top.

Cover the pot and transfer to the oven. Braise the pork belly until very tender, 4 to 4½ hours. Uncover and let the pork belly cool overnight in the braising liquid.

(recipe continues)

The next day, scrape off as much fat from the braising liquid as possible and reserve to make the Smoked Chile Pork Schmaltz (page 169). Remove the pork belly from the braising liquid, and cut into 10 serving pieces, each about a 2-inch cube. Set aside.

Bring the braising liquid to a boil and cook, whisking occasionally, until it has reduced to a sauce and thickened slightly, about 20 minutes. Season the sauce with salt and pepper to taste. Cover to keep warm.

Meanwhile, make the turnip purée: Put the turnips in a medium heavy pot, cover with water, and stir in 1 tablespoon salt. Bring to a boil and cook until the vegetables are very tender, about 30 minutes. Use a slotted spoon to transfer the turnips to a blender. Add the butter and purée until smooth. Season to taste with salt.

Preheat the broiler. Just before serving, place the pork belly cubes on a baking sheet and broil until golden and warmed through. To serve, divide the purée between plates. Top with the pork belly and some of the sauce.

High and low mingle easily at Wyebrook's table: champagne flutes with Mason jar water glasses, beef strip loin with smoked chile pork schmaltz.

ALICOT OF BEEF *with Potato Gnocchi*

Alicot, a type of stew hailing from southern France, cleverly uses poultry giblets like gizzards, livers, necks, and wing tips—in other words, the parts less prized—to create a rich, comforting dish. This version eschews chicken for beef and produces a hearty ragu that transforms the peasant-worthy parts into a king's supper.

SERVES 10 WITH LEFTOVERS

FOR THE ALICOT

1 (2½-pound) beef heart

1 (1½- to 2-pound) beef tongue

2 pounds beef cheeks

1 pound beef liver

Fine sea salt and freshly ground black pepper

½ cup (1 stick) unsalted butter

4 large carrots, chopped

4 celery ribs, chopped

2 medium onions, chopped

8 garlic cloves, finely chopped

6 anchovy filets

3 quarts Rich Chicken Stock (page 246)

FOR THE GNOCCHI

2 pounds russet potatoes

½ cup heavy cream

3 large eggs, lightly beaten

Fine sea salt and freshly ground black pepper

2½ cups all-purpose flour, or as needed

½ cup (1 stick) unsalted butter, melted

¼ cup finely chopped flat-leaf parsley

1 teaspoon finely grated lemon zest

1 garlic clove, finely chopped

Make the alicot: Preheat a grill, preferably with hardwood or hardwood charcoal. Let the fire burn down to coals. Season the heart, tongue, cheeks, and liver generously with salt and pepper, then grill, turning occasionally, until golden brown, about 20 minutes.

Heat the butter in a large heavy pot over medium-high heat until hot, then add the carrots, celery, onions, garlic, 1 teaspoon salt, and ½ teaspoon pepper. Cook, stirring occasionally, until the vegetables are golden, about 10 minutes. Add the anchovy filets and cook, stirring, until they melt into the vegetable mixture. Add the heart, tongue, cheeks, liver, and stock to the pot and bring to a simmer. Simmer, covered, until the meats are very tender, 5 to 6 hours. Remove from the heat and transfer the meats to a large platter and let cool slightly. Reserve the braising liquid.

Chop the liver and purée it in a blender with 3 cups of the braising liquid; set aside. Shred the cheeks with a fork. Peel the tongue and cut the meat into ½-inch pieces. Remove and discard any fat and hard tissue from the heart, then cut into ½-inch pieces.

Return the chopped meats and the puréed liver to the remaining braising liquid in the pot and bring to a simmer. Simmer the alicot until it is a thick ragu, about 1 hour. Season with salt and pepper to taste.

Make the gnocchi: Preheat the oven to 400°F.

Place the potatoes on a baking sheet and bake until tender, about 1 hour. Let the potatoes cool slightly, then peel them and force the flesh through a ricer into a large bowl. Add the cream, eggs, and 1 teaspoon salt, and stir until combined. Stir in 1½ cups flour and knead the dough in the bowl, adding more flour, a little at a time, as you knead. Stop adding flour when the dough comes together and stops sticking to the sides of the bowl. Transfer the dough to a work surface and knead until smooth and elastic, about 6 minutes. Cut the dough into 6 pieces and roll each piece into a 1-inch-thick log. Cut the log crosswise into 1½-inch-long pieces.

Cook the gnocchi in a large pot of boiling salted water. Once the gnocchi float to the surface of the water, cook 2 minutes longer, then remove them with a slotted spoon and transfer to a bowl of ice and cold water.

Before serving, heat 4 tablespoons of the butter in a large heavy skillet or on a griddle, then sauté the gnocchi, in batches if necessary, until golden, about 8 minutes per batch. Toss the gnocchi with the parsley, lemon zest, garlic, and remaining 4 tablespoons butter. Season to taste with salt and pepper. Serve the gnocchi with the alicot.

VANILLA-BAY ROASTED BEEF STRIP LOIN *with Concord Grape Demi Glace and Faux Purple Carrots*

Vanilla, bay, and lavender—spices that we usually associate with sweets—in this beef's savory spice rub enhance the fruitiness of the Concord grape sauce. The carrots that simmer in the grape juice gain a ring of purple and, when sliced, resemble the purple carrots that always lose their color when cooked.

SERVES 10

FOR THE BEEF

3 bay leaves

2 tablespoons coriander seeds

1 tablespoon fresh thyme leaves

1 vanilla bean, cut into pieces

1 teaspoon lavender flowers

½ teaspoon black peppercorns

1 (6- to 7-pound) whole beef strip loin with fat cap attached

Fine sea salt

FOR THE CARROTS AND SAUCE

5 orange carrots, peeled

3 cups Concord grape juice, preferably freshly pressed

2 cups Rich Beef Stock (page 248)

1 tablespoon cornstarch

2 tablespoons water

4 tablespoons unsalted butter

Fine sea salt and freshly ground black pepper

20 baby kale leaves

Prepare the beef: Combine the bay leaves, coriander, thyme, vanilla bean, lavender flowers, and peppercorns in a spice grinder and grind to a powder. Sprinkle the beef with 1 tablespoon salt, rubbing the salt into the meat. Rub the spice mixture all over the beef and let stand at room temperature for 1 hour before roasting.

Preheat the oven to 200°F. Place the beef on a rack set in a roasting pan. Roast the beef until a meat thermometer registers 120°F, 1 to 1½ hours. Let the beef rest at room temperature for 25 minutes. Preheat a griddle over high heat. Sear the beef, fat side down, until golden. Remove from the heat.

Meanwhile, make the sauce and carrots: Place the whole peeled carrots in a saucepan large enough to fit them, then pour the grape juice over the carrots and bring to a simmer over medium-high heat. Simmer the carrots until they are purple and very tender, about 30 minutes.

Remove the carrots and cut them into thick coins. Bring the grape juice to a boil and reduce to 1 cup. Add the stock and continue to boil until the liquid measures 2 cups. Stir the cornstarch into the water until dissolved, then slowly whisk the cornstarch mixture into the boiling sauce until slightly thickened (you may not use all the cornstarch). Remove the saucepan from the heat and whisk in the butter until melted and combined. Season the sauce with salt and pepper to taste.

To serve, thinly slice the beef. Spoon some of the sauce in the middle of a serving plate, then top with the sliced beef. Place the carrots around the beef and garnish the plate with the kale leaves.

CHOCOLATE CAKES
with Port-Soaked Fruit and Crème Anglaise

Each of this dessert's parts can stand alone: The cakes can be served in the summer with fresh strawberries and whipped cream. The fruit makes a boozy-sweet topping for angel food or pound cake, and we won't blame you if you want to lap up the crème anglaise with a spoon. Of course, serving them together makes a dessert fit for the finest of holidays.

SERVES 10

FOR THE CRÈME ANGLAISE

6 large egg yolks

2 cups heavy cream

½ cup sugar

Fine sea salt

1 vanilla bean, split

FOR THE PORT-SOAKED FRUIT

1 cup dried apricots (preferably California), halved

¼ cup golden raisins

¼ cup dried cherries

¼ cup dried cranberries

½ cup sugar

Fine sea salt

2 cups port

FOR THE CHOCOLATE CAKES

1 cup (2 sticks) unsalted butter

8 ounces 60% bittersweet chocolate, chopped

4 large eggs

Fine sea salt

3 tablespoons all-purpose flour

Make the crème anglaise: Whisk together the egg yolks, cream, sugar, and ¼ teaspoon salt in a heavy saucepan. Run the tip of a knife along the cut sides of the vanilla bean, scraping out the seeds, then place the seeds and bean in the cream mixture. Place the saucepan over medium heat and stir constantly with a spatula, scraping the bottom of the saucepan, until the sauce is thick enough to coat the spatula. Remove from the heat and pour through a fine-mesh sieve. Cool the sauce to room temperature to serve. If making ahead, chill with a piece of plastic wrap laid over the surface of the sauce to prevent a skin from forming.

(recipe continues)

Make the port-soaked fruit: Place the apricots, raisins, cherries, cranberries, sugar, and a large pinch of salt in a heavy saucepan then pour the port over top. Bring to a simmer and cook, stirring occasionally, until the liquid has reduced by about half and has become syrupy. Let cool to room temperature, then season to taste with salt. If making ahead, the fruit can be kept, covered, at room temperature for up to 3 days. Refrigerate if keeping longer than 3 days.

Make the chocolate cakes: Preheat the oven to 325°F. Butter 10 (½-cup) muffin cups.

Combine the butter and chocolate in a metal bowl, then place the bowl over a saucepan of barely simmering water. Stir the chocolate mixture occasionally until completely melted, then let cool slightly.

Beat the eggs with ½ teaspoon salt in a separate bowl until well combined. Slowly pour the chocolate mixture into the eggs, whisking to combine. Fold in the flour. Taste the batter and season to taste with salt.

Divide the batter between the buttered muffin cups. Bake the cakes until the edges are set but the centers are still liquid, 15 to 20 minutes. Let the cakes cool slightly, then gently remove them from the muffin tins.

To serve, spoon about ⅓ cup of the crème anglaise into each shallow serving bowl. Place a cake on top of the sauce then spoon the dried fruit and some syrup over each cake.

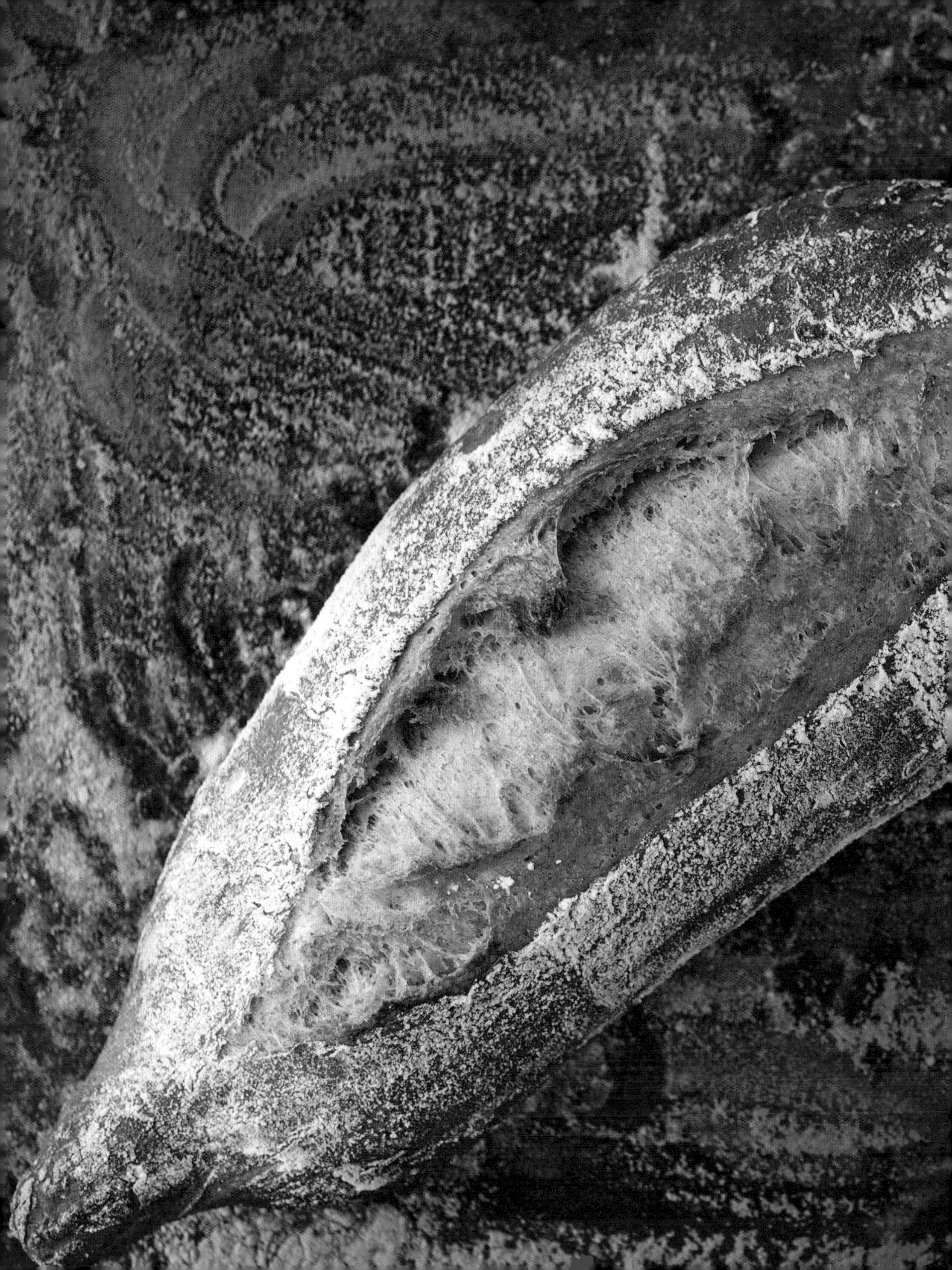

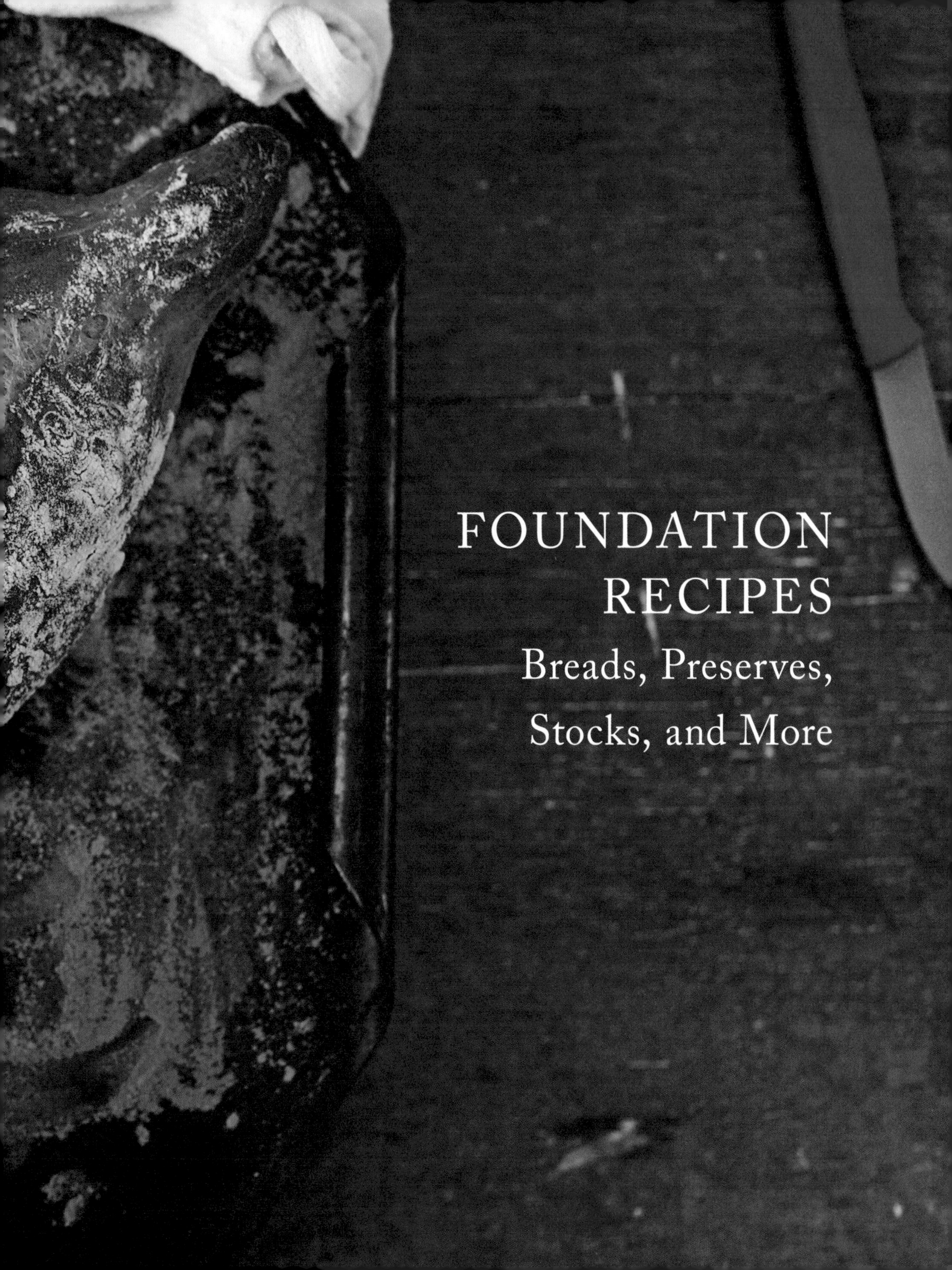

FOUNDATION RECIPES

Breads, Preserves, Stocks, and More

The cook who dies with the best-stocked pantry wins. This is a joke that we toss around the kitchen, especially during the harvest season when we spend days dehydrating, smoking, fermenting, and preserving for the cooler months to come. Except we kind of mean it. We try to put everything up.

The means of extending the season in the kitchen are not new. These techniques come from a time before refrigeration, when you simply could not get your hands on a tomato in February unless you had canned it yourself in August. In our kitchen, the contents of these jars and crocks are more than just preserved ingredients. Through the process, they become their own thing.

The shelves of dried peppers, both sweet and hot, are not just used in the winter, but year-round as unique ingredients in many dishes. Dehydration intensifies the peppers' flavor, revealing an almost caramel sweetness that fresh peppers lack. Pickled vegetables can taste far more complex than their fresh counterparts, and so we may happily pop open a jar of pickled spring radishes even as we are washing the dirt off the first harvest of the season.

The thought of infusing oils and drying spices, roasting and jarring tomatoes, maintaining your own starter and baking bread might feel excessive if you're used to simply buying what you need when you need it. But go ahead and try it, and you too will taste the difference it makes in your food. You'll soon join the ranks of those of us who are stockpiling to win that ultimate prize in the end—and enjoying the fruits of our labors along the way. —*Andrew*

Breads and Pasta

Good bread baking requires more than formula. It demands nurture and understanding. We step into the yeast's world and must give it what it requires, yet have the awareness to know when to intervene. The dough will rise more slowly when cool and faster when warm. Either is fine so long as we can recognize the point at which it must stop. Letting our breads rest for half an hour after an initial mixing gives the flour time to soak up the hydration, enabling the gluten-forming proteins to uncoil so they can link arms when we knead. We are left with a loaf that has improved structure and flavor. After kneading, the dough will rise, sometimes in a warm space, sometimes slowly, coolly, overnight. We bake the loaves. We feed the starter and begin again. There is ritual in baking bread. And there is community in its breaking.

JORGE THE SOURDOUGH STARTER

Named by our first in-house baker, Jorge is the foundation for many of our breads. He is similar to the starter used by the esteemed chef Nancy Silverton, who captures the wild yeast found naturally on grape skins—take care not to wash that bloom of yeast away before you get started. We've added additional fermenting power via raisins for an active starter with a gentle sourness. If you bake less than once a week, you can keep your Jorge active by feeding him every so often. Bonus: Bread made with a sourdough starter lasts a phenomenally long time—much longer than store-bought bread.

MAKES ABOUT 2 CUPS

FOR THE INITIAL FERMENTATION

8 ounces unwashed organic red grapes, stemmed

½ cup organic unsulphured raisins

2½ cups water

2 cups bread flour

FOR FEEDING THE STARTER

1 cup all-purpose flour

1 cup water

Start the initial fermentation: Place the grapes and raisins on several layers of cheesecloth, then gather the corners together and tie to form a bag. Squeeze the bag to lightly crush the grapes.

Whisk the water and flour together in a bowl, then add the grape bag and stir to combine. Cover the bowl with plastic wrap and let stand at warm room temperature, stirring once or twice a day, for 6 days. The mixture should be bubbly and look like it is separating slightly.

Remove the grape bag and squeeze any juice back into the starter. Discard half the starter then transfer the remaining starter to a clean container.

(First-time bakers always have some trepidation about throwing away half the starter, but there is a good reason for it. Jorge isn't strong enough just yet to leaven bread, and by discarding half of him at this point you make him work harder when you introduce more flour and water. Not to mention, you'd run out of space if you just kept feeding him! Don't worry, there will be plenty of Jorge to go around.)

Feed the starter: Stir together 1 cup all-purpose flour and 1 cup water until completely smooth, then stir into the starter. Let the starter stand, covered, at warm room temperature for 4 hours, then refrigerate overnight.

Repeat the process of discarding half the starter and feeding with 1 cup each flour and water for 2 more days, refrigerating overnight each time. The starter is now ready to use.

If fed regularly, the starter will keep indefinitely in the refrigerator (and grow more complex over time). Replace the amount of starter you use with equal parts flour and water, or discard half the starter each week and replace with equal parts flour and water.

COUNTRY WHEAT BATARDS

Whole wheat flour lends a mild nuttiness to these batard-shaped loaves, and their nice dense crumb makes them perfect for toasting.

MAKES 2 LOAVES

3⅓ cups warm water

1 cup Jorge the Sourdough Starter (page 196) or ½ ounce fresh yeast

6⅓ cups bread flour

1⅔ cups whole wheat flour

2 tablespoons, plus 1 teaspoon fine sea salt

Place the water and Jorge in the bowl of a stand mixer fitted with a dough hook. Add the bread flour and whole wheat flour, then mix on low speed until just combined. Let the mixture stand for 30 minutes.

Add the salt then knead the dough in the mixer on high speed until it is very elastic, about 10 minutes. Place the dough on a floured work surface and shape into a round by pulling the outer edges up and into the center of the round, working all the way around the dough. Place the dough back in the bowl and cover with a kitchen towel. Let rise at warm room temperature until doubled in size, 2 to 3 hours.

Turn the dough out onto a floured work surface and divide in half. Pat each piece of dough into a rectangle. Pull one long edge of dough away from the center of the dough, stretching it, then fold the edge along and into the center of the dough, pressing down. Repeat this shaping on the other long side of the dough to form a 12 x 6-inch oval. Pull the ends of the loaf out and squeeze them into points. Repeat with the remaining piece of dough. Place the loaves, seam side down, on a floured baking sheet. Dust the loaves with flour, cover with a kitchen towel, and let rise a second time until the dough doubles in size, about 1½ hours.

Preheat the oven to 450°F. Dust the loaves with flour and slash the dough down the center with a razor blade.

Place 3 ice cubes on the bottom of the oven. Bake the bread until golden brown and hollow-sounding when tapped, 45 minutes to 1 hour. Transfer the bread to rack and let cool completely before slicing.

WHOLE WHEAT SOURDOUGH BREAD

We use a combination of sourdough starter and yeast to produce a mild sourness that won't overwhelm this hearty loaf's nuanced whole wheat flavor. A smear of good butter really seals the deal.

MAKES 1 LOAF

1⅓ cups warm water

⅓ cup Jorge the Sourdough Starter (page 196)

2½ tablespoons honey or Grade B maple syrup

2 teaspoons active dry yeast

2¾ cups whole wheat flour

1¼ cups bread flour

2½ teaspoons fine sea salt

Place the water, Jorge, honey, and yeast in the bowl of a stand mixer fitted with the paddle attachment, then mix on low speed to combine. Add the flours and mix on low speed until just combined. Let the mixture stand for 30 minutes.

Add the salt then knead the dough in the mixer on high speed until very elastic, about 10 minutes. Place the dough on a floured work surface and shape into a round by pulling the outer edges up and into the center of the round, working all the way around the dough. Place the dough back in the bowl and cover with a kitchen towel. Let the dough rise at warm room temperature until doubled in size, about 2 hours.

Place the dough on a floured work surface and shape into a round again by pulling the outer edges up and into the center of the round, working all the way around the dough. Place the dough, seam side down, on a floured baking sheet. Dust the dough with flour, then cover with a kitchen towel and let rise a second time until the dough doubles in size, about 1 hour.

Preheat the oven to 450°F. Dust the surface of the loaf with flour and slash the dough with a razor blade.

Place 3 ice cubes on the bottom of the oven. Bake the bread until golden brown and hollow-sounding when tapped, 45 minutes to 1 hour. Transfer the bread to a rack to cool completely before slicing.

Country Wheat Batard

Crackling-Studded Pullman Loaf

Buttermilk Sourdough
Pan d'Epi
Whole Wheat
Sourdough Bread

BUTTERMILK SOURDOUGH PAN D'EPI

An overnight ferment of buttermilk and yeast (called a poolish in bakers' circles) lends a gentle sour to this baguette shaped like a wheat stalk.

MAKES 2 LOAVES

1 cup buttermilk

A large pinch of active dry or fresh yeast

4¼ cups all-purpose flour

¾ cup warm water

1 tablespoon fine sea salt

Whisk together the buttermilk, yeast, and 1 cup of the flour in a medium bowl. Let the mixture stand, covered, overnight in a warm place.

Stir in the water, salt, and the remaining 3¼ cups flour until a wet dough forms. Transfer the dough to a work surface and knead until the dough is smooth and elastic, about 10 minutes. Place the dough back in the bowl, cover with a kitchen towel, and let rise in a warm place until doubled in size, about 2 hours.

Turn the dough out onto a lightly floured work surface and divide in half. With a long side of one piece of dough in front of you, fold the outer edge into the center from left to right, pressing down and stretching as you fold. Repeat this movement on the other edge, folding it into the center to begin to form a long loaf. Repeat until the loaf fits the length of a baking sheet. Transfer the loaf to a floured baking sheet, seam side down, and repeat with the remaining dough. Dust the loaves with flour and let rise, covered with a kitchen towel, until they double in size, about 1 hour.

Preheat the oven to 475°F. Use kitchen shears to cut the loaves into the wheat stalk shape: Holding the shears at a 30° angle and starting at one end of the baguette, cut through the dough almost to the bottom, then lift the cut dough and pull it gently to one side. Make the next cut and pull the dough to the opposite side of the loaf. Continue cutting the entire length of the loaf in this manner. Repeat with the remaining loaf.

Bake the loaves until they are dark golden brown and hollow-sounding when tapped, 35 to 45 minutes. Transfer the loaves to a rack and cool completely.

CRACKLING-STUDDED PULLMAN LOAF

Pullman loaves became popular in the late 1800s because their long square shape allowed them to be stacked easily in narrow train car kitchens. We started baking charcuterie trimmings into the dough as a way to repurpose any leftover nubs after the meat and cheese plates are made. Toasted, this bread makes a spectacular base for a BLT.

MAKES 1 LOAF

1 tablespoon rendered animal fat

¼ cup finely chopped mixed charcuterie such as prosciutto, coppa, speck, bacon, and salami

1 small garlic clove, finely chopped

7 ounces warm water (¾ cup plus 2 tablespoons)

5 ounces warm milk (½ cup plus 2 tablespoons)

1 (¼-ounce) package active dry yeast or ½ ounce fresh yeast

¼ cup sugar

4⅓ cups bread flour

1¾ teaspoons fine sea salt

1 large egg, at room temperature

2 tablespoons unsalted butter, melted and cooled

EQUIPMENT: **A 13 x 4 x 4-inch Pullman loaf pan with a lid**

Heat the rendered fat in a small heavy skillet over medium heat until hot. Stir in the charcuterie and garlic and cook, stirring, until browned and crisp, about 6 minutes. Let the cracklings cool to room temperature.

Combine the water, milk, yeast, and sugar in the bowl of a stand mixer fitted with the paddle attachment and let proof until bubbling, about 5 minutes. Add the bread flour, salt, egg, butter, and reserved cracklings, along with any remaining fat in the skillet, then mix on low speed until just combined. Let the dough mixture stand for 30 minutes.

Knead the dough in the mixer on high speed until very elastic, 8 to 10 minutes. Place the dough on a floured work surface and shape into a round by pulling the outer

Wyebrook's patch of land in southeastern Pennsylvania experiences the seasons fully—from winter's chill to the humid, green extravagance of spring and summer.

edges up and into the center of the round, working all the way around the dough. Place the dough back in the bowl and cover with a kitchen towel. Let the dough rise at warm room temperature until doubled in size, 1 to 2 hours.

Butter the inside of the Pullman loaf pan, including the lid. Turn the dough out onto a floured work surface and pat into a rectangle. Pull one long edge of dough away from the center of the dough, stretching it, then fold the edge along and into the center of the dough rectangle, pressing down. Repeat this movement on the other long side of the dough to form a 13 x 4-inch rectangle of dough. Place the dough, seam side down, in the buttered Pullman loaf pan. Cover the pan with a kitchen towel and let rise a second time until the dough fills the pan, about 1 hour.

Preheat the oven to 375°F.

Slide the Pullman pan lid over the pan then bake until the bread is set, about 25 minutes. Uncover the pan and bake until the crust is dark golden brown and the loaf is hollow-sounding when tapped, 20 to 25 minutes more. Transfer the bread to a rack and let cool completely before slicing.

FRESH PASTA DOUGH

If you've made pasta dough before, this luxurious version, with its deep golden color and fine texture might surprise you, but it makes for a superbly tender and versatile pasta. We use this dough for fettuccine, spaghetti, ravioli, and more. The quality of the eggs here makes a huge difference. Use the best and freshest you can find.

MAKES ABOUT 1¾ POUNDS

12 large egg yolks
3 to 4 large whole eggs
4 cups all-purpose flour

Beat the yolks and 3 of the whole eggs together in a stand mixer using the whisk attachment until combined. Switch to the dough hook and, with the motor running add the flour, 1 cup at a time. Knead the dough in the mixer until it comes together and no longer sticks to the side of the bowl, about 6 minutes. If the dough is too dry and will not come together, add the additional egg. Shape the dough into a ball and wrap in plastic wrap. Let the dough rest at room temperature for 1 hour.

Cut the dough into 2-ounce pieces and cover with a kitchen towel. Roll out one piece of dough using a pasta roller set on the widest setting. Fold the dough in thirds, like a letter, then roll through the widest setting again. Repeat this folding and rolling on the widest setting 4 more times. Change the setting on the pasta roller to the next narrowest setting and roll the dough through once without folding. Continue changing the setting on the pasta roller, making it narrower each time, and rolling the dough through without folding until you reach the desired thickness. Repeat with the remaining pieces of dough.

To make spaghetti: Roll the pasta sheets until they are about 1⁄16th-inch thick (this is about setting 4 on most machines). Roll the pasta sheets through a ⅛-inch pasta cutter to cut into spaghetti. If you're not cooking the pasta right away, hang it over a long dowel or clean broom handle balanced over 2 chairs, and let stand until dry, about 4 hours. Once dried, place the pasta in a sealed container and store at room temperature for 1 week or freeze for a month or more.

To make fettuccine: Roll the pasta sheets until you can just see a work surface through them when they are laid flat on the surface (this is about setting 6 on most machines). Roll the pasta sheets through a ¼-inch pasta cutter to cut into fettuccine. If you're not cooking the pasta right away, hang it over a long dowel or clean broom handle balanced over 2 chairs, and let stand until dry, about 4 hours. Once dried, place the pasta in a sealed container and store at room temperature for 1 week or freeze for a month or more.

To make pappardelle: Roll the pasta sheets until you can see a work surface through them when they are laid flat on the surface (this is about setting 6 on most machines). Using a sharp knife, cut the sheet lengthwise into 1-inch wide noodles. If you're not cooking the pasta right away, hang it over a dowel or clean broom handle balanced over 2 chairs, and let stand until dry, about 4 hours. Once dried, place the pasta in a sealed container and store at room temperature for 1 week or freeze for a month or more.

To make ravioli: Roll the pasta sheets until you can see a work surface through them when they are laid flat on the surface (this is about setting 7 on most machines). Fill with ravioli filling, top with another sheet of pasta, and seal immediately. Uncooked ravioli can be arranged on a baking sheet in a single layer and frozen. Transfer to a resealable plastic bag and store in the freezer for up to 1 month.

PICI PASTA

These thick, chewy, handrolled noodles should be cooked as soon as they are made. They are perfect for rich, clinging, meaty sauces like our Goat, Tomato, and Green Coriander Ragu (page 132).

MAKES ABOUT 2 POUNDS

2 cups semolina flour

2 cups all-purpose flour

Fine sea salt

1 to 1¼ cups warm water

Stir together the semolina and all-purpose flours in a large bowl with 1 teaspoon salt. Add 1 cup water and stir until a dough forms. If the dough is too dry, add more water a little at a time until it comes together but is not sticky. Transfer the dough to a work surface and knead it with your hands until it is smooth and elastic, about 8 minutes. Wrap the dough in plastic wrap and let stand at room temperature for 15 minutes.

Cut the dough into 32 equal pieces. Roll 1 piece of dough between your hands or on an unfloured work surface to create a long, snake-like noodle, about ¼-inch-thick. Place the pici on a baking sheet that has been dusted with semolina flour and cover the pasta with a clean dish towel. Repeat with the remaining dough. Set aside until ready to use.

Preserves, Sauces, and Ferments

We take fruits and vegetables when they are ripe and fresh and save them for the times when they are not. Yes, a refrigerator might do for a while, but a three-month old head of cauliflower or cabbage does not improve with age. But a fermented cauliflower pickle does. So does sauerkraut. A red onion has a long shelf life even without the fridge. And red onions are good. But pickled red onions are better. We pluck ripe tomatoes from the vines, save them in jars, and whirl them into tomato mustards. Pulling a jar of homemade tomato sauce from the pantry is better than using out-of-season tomatoes—the fruit's goodness has been preserved at its peak. We are not breaking new ground but treading old ground, and we are eating better, all year, because of it.

PICKLED MUSTARD SEEDS

This first step in mustard making lets the seeds' enzymes begin to activate. They puff and pop like caviar when you bite down on them. We go on to whiz them into all sorts of mustard variations, but they're a great garnish on their own.

MAKES ABOUT 1 QUART

1 cup yellow mustard seeds

1 cup brown mustard seeds

2 cups water

⅔ cup apple cider vinegar or red wine vinegar

Fine sea salt

Combine the mustard seeds, water, and vinegar in a bowl and let stand, uncovered, at room temperature until the mixture begins to thicken and become slightly viscous, 24 to 48 hours. Transfer to an airtight container and refrigerate until ready to use. Pickled mustard seeds will keep for several months. Season to taste with salt before using.

DIJON-STYLE MUSTARD

This coarse, country-style mustard has a sharp bite to it, so tread lightly until you know your tolerance level. For a smoother texture, add 2 tablespoons white wine as you blend and let the motor run for longer than you feel comfortable—try a full minute to start.

MAKES ABOUT 1 QUART

1 quart Pickled Mustard Seeds made with red wine vinegar (page 212)

Fine sea salt

2 to 3 tablespoons grade B maple syrup

Combine the pickled mustard seeds, 4 teaspoons salt, and maple syrup to taste in a blender and purée until very smooth. Taste and adjust the seasonings. The mustard keeps, refrigerated in an airtight container, for several months.

CREOLE MUSTARD

As the dried sweet peppers in this mustard rehydrate, their color intensifies, but don't let that pretty sunset hue fool you—this condiment packs a spicy punch.

MAKES ABOUT 2 CUPS

2 cups Pickled Mustard Seeds made with apple cider vinegar (page 212)

⅓ cup Dehydrated Sweet Peppers (page 239)

1 tablespoon Pennsylvania Chile Sauce (page 233)

Fine sea salt

Combine the pickled mustard seeds, dehydrated sweet peppers, chile sauce, and 1 tablespoon salt in a food processor and pulse until coarsely ground. Season to taste with salt. Creole mustard keeps refrigerated in an airtight container for several months.

HORSERADISH MUSTARD CREAM

This simple sauce is a natural with Smoked Pork Loin (page 32) and makes a welcome substitute for sour cream for Beef Cheek Borscht (page 68). It's also a fantastic addition to just about any sandwich, so keep some at the ready in your fridge at all times.

MAKES ABOUT 1¼ CUPS

1 cup sour cream

3 tablespoons freshly grated horseradish

2 tablespoons Pickled Mustard Seeds (page 212)

Fine sea salt and freshly ground black pepper

Stir together the sour cream, horseradish, pickled mustard seeds, ½ teaspoon salt, and ¼ teaspoon pepper. Taste and adjust the seasonings. The horseradish-mustard cream keeps for up to 1 month in a sealed container in the refrigerator.

ROASTED TOMATO AND MUSTARD RELISH

We whip up this versatile condiment every tomato season and smear it on meats like our Merguez Sausage (page 117) or Super-Crust Spatchcocked Chicken (page 140). But it's flavorful enough to stand in as a quick sauce when tossed with simple buttered noodles.

MAKES ABOUT 2 CUPS

1 pound ripe plum tomatoes

1 tablespoon extra-virgin olive oil

¼ cup Dijon-Style Mustard (page 214)

Fine sea salt

Preheat the oven to 425°F. Halve the tomatoes lengthwise. Toss the tomatoes with the oil, then place on a baking sheet and roast in the oven until very tender and browned in places, 35 to 45 minutes. Let the tomatoes cool slightly, then slip off and discard their skins. Place the tomatoes and any juices in a bowl, then mash together with the mustard. Season to taste with salt. The relish keeps, refrigerated in an airtight container, for up to 2 weeks.

PLUM MUSTARD RELISH

You'll want to keep this spicy-sweet condiment in heavy rotation, especially through plum season. It's a lively addition to Goat in Hay (page 126) or to any cheese board.

MAKES ABOUT 1½ CUPS

1 pound ripe plums
1 tablespoon Grade B maple syrup
⅓ cup Creole Mustard (page 214)
Fine sea salt

Preheat the oven to 425°F. Halve the plums lengthwise, discarding the pits. Toss the plums with the maple syrup then place on a baking sheet and roast in the oven until very tender and browned in places, about 25 minutes. Let the plums cool slightly, then slip off and discard their skins. Place the plums and any juices in a bowl, then mash together with the Creole mustard. Season to taste with salt. The relish keeps, refrigerated in an airtight container, for at least 2 weeks.

GIARDINIERA

This recipe for pickled garden vegetables is pretty close to the Italian classic, but feel free to experiment. We make it throughout the growing season with whatever happens to be fresh. The springtime version might contain green beans and radishes, while the fall variety might feature Swiss chard stems and turnips.

MAKES ABOUT 1 GALLON

1 pound carrots, chopped

1 bunch celery, chopped

2 red bell peppers, stemmed, seeded, and cut into strips

1 head cauliflower, trimmed and chopped

1 onion, sliced

2 garlic cloves, thinly sliced

1 fresh hot green chile, thinly sliced

8 cups warm water

Fine sea salt

EQUIPMENT: **A large clean crock or jar**

Place the vegetables, garlic, and chile in a cleaned crock or large glass jar. Stir together the water and 6 tablespoons salt until the salt is dissolved. Pour the brine over the vegetables. Fill a resealable plastic bag half full with water, then seal the bag. Place the water bag on top of the vegetables to keep them submerged beneath the brine.

Let the giardiniera ferment at room temperature until sufficiently sour, at least 2 weeks and up to 1 month. Chill the giardiniera in the brine, covered, until ready to use. Giardiniera keeps, chilled, for at least 4 months.

CIPPOLINI AGRODOLCE

Local maple syrup provides the sweetness in this spin on the Italian classic—use the darkest, most flavorful stuff you can find. The sour component comes from apple cider vinegar, and the combination of the two is a pathway to the old continent via the American northeast.

MAKES ABOUT 3 CUPS

1 pound small red or white cippolini onions

¼ cup extra-virgin olive oil

2 bay leaves

½ cup apple cider vinegar

½ cup Grade B maple syrup

Fine sea salt

Cook the onions in simmering water until they are just tender, about 8 minutes. Drain the onions and let cool. Trim and peel the onions, leaving them whole.

Heat the oil and bay leaves in a large heavy skillet over medium-high heat until hot. Add the onions and cook, stirring occasionally, until they are golden brown, about 4 minutes. Stir in the vinegar, maple syrup, and ¾ teaspoon salt and cook, stirring, until the liquid has started to caramelize, 2 to 3 minutes. Let cool to room temperature and season with salt to taste. Stored in an airtight container in the refrigerator, the onions will keep for up to 1 month.

SAUERKRAUT

Like Giardiniera (page 219), our sauerkraut relies on lactic fermentation to produce its distinctive sour flavor. We add enough salt to a brine to keep airborne critters from spoiling the lot and let the cabbage ferment at room temperature until it's sour enough for our liking—at least 1 week and up to a month.

MAKES ABOUT 2 QUARTS

5 pounds green cabbage

Fine sea salt

EQUIPMENT: **A large clean crock or jar**

Core the cabbage, then thinly slice it and toss with 3 tablespoons salt in a large bowl. Using a meat pounder or a cleaned empty wine bottle, pound and crush the cabbage for several minutes, until a brine starts to form from the released liquid. Transfer the cabbage along with the brine to a crock, pressing down so that the brine completely covers the cabbage. Place a plate or a resealable plastic bag filled with water on top of the cabbage to keep it submerged.

Let the cabbage ferment at cool room temperature until sour. Taste the sauerkraut after 1 week. If you are happy with its taste and texture, transfer the sauerkraut to a sealed container and refrigerate. If you prefer a more sour flavor and tender texture, let the sauerkraut continue to ferment at room temperature for up to 1 month before refrigerating. Refrigerated, the sauerkraut will keep for months.

PICKLED RED ONIONS

Pickled red onions should be a standard in every kitchen. They are easy to make, keep well in the fridge, and are delicious on just about everything.

MAKES ABOUT 1 QUART

1½ cups apple cider vinegar
1½ cups water
3 tablespoons Grade B maple syrup
Fine sea salt
1½ pounds red onions, thinly sliced

Combine the vinegar, water, maple syrup, and 1½ tablespoons salt in a saucepan and bring to a boil, stirring until the salt is dissolved. Remove the saucepan from the heat, then stir in the onions. Let the mixture stand at room temperature until cool, then transfer to a sealed container. Pickled red onions keep, refrigerated in an airtight container, for at least 1 month.

SPRING PICKLES

The first bright, fresh vegetables of the year offer such sweet relief after a long, hard winter. We like to pack spring's early edibles in jars so we can experience that blessed feeling all year.

MAKES ABOUT 3 PINTS

1½ cups apple cider vinegar

½ cup water

⅓ cup sugar

1 tablespoon pickling spices

1 bay leaf

Fine sea salt

2 bunches radishes, trimmed and halved lengthwise

2 bunches ramps, trimmed

1 cup cleaned fiddlehead ferns

Combine the vinegar, water, sugar, pickling spices, bay leaf, and 2 tablespoons salt in a small saucepan and bring to a boil, stirring until the sugar is dissolved. Remove from the heat and let cool slightly.

Divide the radishes, ramps, and fiddlehead ferns among 3 sterilized pint jars, then pour the pickling liquid over the vegetables to cover, leaving a ½-inch of space at the top of each jar. Seal the jars and process in a hot water bath for 30 minutes. Let the jars cool to room temperature until they seal. Spring pickles keep in a cool, dry pantry for up to 1 year.

ROASTED TOMATO PURÉE

We can all agree that tomatoes are only delicious during the summer months, right? When we're not eating them raw and juicy, we roast perfectly ripe tomatoes to further intensify their summery sunshine then preserve them in jars for later use. Popping one open in January is a real treat.

MAKES 3 QUARTS

15 pounds ripe tomatoes, such as Roma or beefsteak

Fine sea salt

Preheat the oven to 400°F. Halve the tomatoes, then place them, cut side down, on baking sheets. Roast the tomatoes in the oven until most of the juice they release has evaporated and their skins are loose, 35 to 55 minutes, depending on the size of the tomatoes. Let them cool slightly, slip off and discard their skins, then transfer the tomatoes along with any juices to a blender. Add 1 tablespoon salt and purée until smooth.

Divide the purée among sterilized jars, then process in a hot water bath for at least 10 minutes. Let the jars cool to room temperature until they seal. Roasted tomato purée keeps in a cool, dry pantry for up to 1 year.

CANNING 101

It should really be called jarring, since that's what we use, but popular nomenclature labels the act of preserving vegetable in jars "canning." This technique works for any high-acid food. If you're looking to preserve meats or low-acid foods, you'll want to invest in a pressure canner.

THE EQUIPMENT

Canning jars

Canning lids with a rubber ring that seals the lids to the jars

Metal screw bands

A large pot or canner

A jar grabber or a pair of tongs

A lid lifter

A jar funnel

Wash the jars, lids, and rings with soap and hot water and rinse well. Place the jars and lids in the pot and cover with water, then bring to a boil. Transfer the jars and lids to a work surface lined with clean kitchen towels to dry.

Fill the jars, leaving a ½-inch of air space at the top. Wipe off the rim of the jars with a clean, damp towel then place the lids and metal screw bands on the jars, tightening the screw bands.

Place the jars back in the pot and cover with water. Bring them back to a boil and process for at least 10 minutes to seal the jars. Transfer the jars to a work surface to cool.

Press the center of each lid to make sure it has sealed. Refrigerate any jars that have not sealed and use them first. The sealed jars can be stored in a cool, dry, dark place for up to a year.

PENNSYLVANIA CHILE SAUCE

This hot sauce uses a blend of different chiles from local Chester County farms: fatali, habanero, Scotch bonnet, cayenne, and more. Each chile has a unique flavor and heat, and when combined, they become something really special. This recipe, which mellows considerably with age, makes enough to keep for a year.

MAKES ABOUT 2 PINTS

12 ounces fresh hot red, orange, and yellow chiles, stemmed and halved

1 head roasted garlic, cloves peeled

2¼ cups apple cider vinegar

2 tablespoons Grade B maple syrup

Fine sea salt

Pulse the chiles and garlic in a food processor until finely chopped. Put the vinegar, maple syrup, and 1 tablespoon salt in a medium saucepan and bring to a boil. Add the chiles and return to a boil. Remove from the heat and let cool.

Divide the hot sauce between sterilized canning jars, then process in a hot water bath for at least 10 minutes. Let the jars cool to room temperature until they seal. The sauce keeps in a cool, dry pantry for up to 1 year. If you do not process the jars, keep them refrigerated until you're ready to use them.

CHILE OIL

This chile oil has a mild kick that livens up everything from pasta sauce to sandwiches. But it's transformative when drizzled on Nervetti Salad (page 83), rounding out the flavor and providing a nice back-of-the-throat warmth.

MAKES ABOUT 1 CUP

½ cup mixed dried chiles, such as cayenne, malagueta, cherry, and red poblano

1 cup extra-virgin olive oil

Lightly crush the chiles then combine them with the oil and place in a warm spot (about 150°F), such as an oven with the pilot on, overnight. Drain and discard the chiles. Chile oil keeps in an airtight container at cool room temperature for at least a month.

LEMON-INFUSED OLIVE OIL

If you come across a recipe that calls for lemon juice but not the zest, use a vegetable peeler to cut thin strips of peel before you juice the fruit. Tuck the zest in a jar of olive oil to make an infused oil that is great for drizzling or in vinaigrettes.

MAKES ABOUT 1 CUP

1 cup extra-virgin olive oil

About 6 strips lemon zest

Combine the oil and zest in a glass container with a lid and let infuse at room temperature for 24 hours. Discard the zest before using.

CANDIED VALENCIA ORANGES

This recipe, based on a classic Mediterranean preserving technique, produces a rich, lightly caramelized syrup full of tender fruit that you can eat skins and all. You can use any number of oranges for this recipe, but keep in mind that you'll want an equal weight of oranges and sugar.

MAKES ABOUT 3 CUPS

3 Valencia oranges (1¼ pounds), thinly sliced crosswise

2¾ cups sugar

Combine the orange slices and sugar in a medium heavy saucepan and heat over low heat until the mixture registers 200°F on a candy thermometer. Continue to cook the oranges at 200°F until they are very tender and the liquid has formed a syrup, about 24 hours. (You can stop this process at any point, continuing where you left off the next day.) Let the candied oranges cool completely in the syrup, then refrigerate until ready to use.

Dried Pantry Goods

Removing the moisture from vegetables and seeds is not just a tried and true method for preservation but also a way to magnify a food's delicate essence. These flavors are often contained in sugars and volatile oils, both quite sensitive to heat. Just a few degrees too high, and sweet peppers will start to toast instead of dehydrate; spices will become tasteless. A dehydrator is a worthwhile tool, but a very low oven will suffice in many cases. Once completely dry, seal your goods and store them away from light and excessive moisture.

DRIED GREEN CORIANDER

The golden brown coriander seeds that you find in the supermarket spice aisle are harvested after the seeds dry naturally on the plant. Green coriander seeds are plucked after the plant flowers but before they dry. At this point, the seeds are still smooth-skinned and green, with a bright flavor closer to cilantro than what we're used to from the completely dried seeds.

MAKES ½ CUP

½ cup green coriander seeds

Spread the coriander seeds out in one layer on a tray and let dry completely at room temperature. Store the coriander seeds, sealed, in a cool, dry place.

DEHYDRATED SWEET PEPPERS

We use deep red Topepo Rosso peppers for their sweetness and low water content, which means they dehydrate relatively quickly. We add the dried peppers to sauces and braises throughout the year. Use this same technique for drying whole hot chiles (but don't remove the seeds and ribs, where much of the heat is found).

MAKES ABOUT 2 CUPS

6 ripe sweet peppers, preferably Topepo Rosso

Use a dehydrator or preheat the oven to its very lowest setting. Halve the peppers. Remove and discard the stems, seeds, and ribs. Coarsely chop the peppers, then place them in the dehydrator or on a baking sheet in the oven with the door ajar, and dehydrate completely, 8 to 12 hours. Sealed in an airtight container and stored in a cool, dry place, the dried peppers will keep for several months.

FRESH RICOTTA CHEESE

We used to make our ricotta with vinegar instead of lemon juice, but found the resulting whey slightly astringent and not so great to cook with—even though throwing it out felt like such a waste. Now we use lemon juice, which makes for a slightly sweet whey that we can repurpose in all sorts of dishes, and the cheese benefits from that slight citrus note. Don't skimp on the cream—this cheese is extra luscious because of it.

MAKES ABOUT 2 QUARTS RICOTTA AND 3 QUARTS WHEY

1 gallon whole milk

4 cups heavy cream

Fine sea salt

½ cup freshly squeezed lemon juice

Combine the milk, cream, and ½ teaspoon salt in a large heavy pot, then place over medium heat and, stirring frequently, bring to 190°F. Remove the pot from the heat and whisk in the lemon juice. Let the mixture stand undisturbed until the curds and whey have separated, about 15 minutes.

Line a sieve with 3 layers of cheesecloth and set over a large bowl. Ladle the curds into the sieve, then gather together the edges of the cheesecloth to form a sack. Tie the edges of the cheesecloth around a wooden spoon, then hang the cheesecloth over the bowl and let it drain completely, about 3 hours.

Transfer the ricotta to a container and refrigerate until ready to use. Transfer the whey to a separate container and save for another use. Both the ricotta and whey will keep, refrigerated, for up to 2 weeks.

11 12 16 17 18 19 20

GARLIC CONFIT

A container of garlic confit in the fridge is like money in the bank. The soft cloves add richness to all kinds of dishes and are fantastic by themselves, smeared on toast. But that's only half the joy—the butter becomes more than itself in the exchange, too. Use it in combination with olive oil for searing chicken or lamb or for making garlic bread.

MAKES 6 HEADS OF GARLIC CONFIT AND 1 POUND OF GARLIC BUTTER

6 heads garlic, separated into cloves
1 pound unsalted butter

Place the unpeeled garlic cloves and butter in a small heavy saucepan and bring to a bare simmer over low heat. Gently cook the garlic until very soft, about 1 hour. (If the garlic starts to brown, lower the heat.) Strain the garlic, collecting the butter in a bowl. Transfer the garlic and the butter to separate airtight containers and refrigerate until ready to use.

Stocks and Brines

In every great kitchen or cooking school, the road to becoming a fine cook starts with the study of stock. With some knowhow and technique, the cook can empower plain water to become bright with herb and balanced with vegetable, fathomed with flavor and thick with texture. Stock requires some attention, but not too much. There is some obligatory skimming, but only of foam and never of fat. There is seasoning with salt, but just a little. And peppercorns, left whole so as not to become sharp. A great stock is made with specific parts, not just any old bones. And then, after it is all it can become, we make it more by making it less. Reduction intensifies and solidifies stock's flavor and body. When your stock is rich enough, let it cool completely, uncovered so it will not turn on you, then cover it and keep it chilled or frozen until you're ready to use its stored power in your cooking.

RICH PORK STOCK

Pork stock is underrated. The amount of gelatin and collagen that comes out of the bones and connective tissue is enough to make the stock stand stiff at room temperature. The mouthfeel this produces is rich beyond most other stocks. If you have trouble finding a pig's head and trotters you can substitute 10 pounds of meaty (but not too fatty) pork bones.

MAKES ABOUT 1 GALLON

1 pig's head, skin and meat removed and reserved (see Pig's Head Torchon, page 41) and halved if possible

4 pork trotters, split lengthwise

3 large onions, unpeeled and quartered

6 celery ribs, trimmed and cut into large pieces

6 carrots, peeled

½ bunch parsley

6 bay leaves

1 tablespoon black peppercorns

Fine sea salt

Place the head, trotters, onions, celery, carrots, parsley, bay leaves, peppercorns, and ½ teaspoon salt in a large stockpot. Add enough water just to cover. Bring the stock to a gentle simmer, skimming any foam from the surface, and let simmer, gently, for 2 hours.

Strain the stock, discarding the solids then place the stock back in the cleaned pot. Boil the stock until it is reduced to 1 gallon. Cool the stock completely, then refrigerate or freeze until ready to use.

RICH CHICKEN STOCK

This stock calls for whole chickens instead of just bones or parts like wings and backs. That might seem excessive, but the result is far richer and fuller than any other method. After the solids are strained, the stock is reduced to make it twice as rich as it began.

MAKES ABOUT 1 GALLON

3 whole chickens

4 large onions, skin on and quartered

1 head celery, trimmed and cut into large pieces

1 pound carrots, peeled

1 bunch parsley

6 bay leaves

1 tablespoon black peppercorns

Fine sea salt

Place the chickens, onions, celery, carrots, parsley, bay leaves, peppercorns, and ½ teaspoon salt in a large stockpot. Add enough water just to cover. Bring the stock to a gentle simmer, skimming any foam from the surface, and let simmer, gently, for 2 hours.

Strain the stock, discarding the solids, then place the stock back in the cleaned pot. Boil the stock until it is reduced to 1 gallon. Cool the stock completely then refrigerate or freeze until ready to use.

RICH BEEF STOCK

Roasting the bones and vegetables before they go in the stockpot makes for a deeply intense stock. A little tomato paste adds balance and just the right kind of sweetness.

MAKES ABOUT 1 GALLON

10 pounds beef neck and knuckle bones

4 large onions, unpeeled and quartered

1 head celery, trimmed and cut into large pieces

1 pound carrots, peeled

½ cup tomato paste

1 bunch parsley

6 bay leaves

1 tablespoon black peppercorns

Fine sea salt

Preheat the oven to 475°F. Arrange the bones on baking sheets and roast in the oven until well browned, about 45 minutes. Place the bones in a large stockpot. Do not clean the baking sheets.

Combine the onions, celery, and carrots on the baking sheets and toss to coat with any remaining fat. Roast the vegetables until golden, 25 to 30 minutes.

Transfer the vegetables to the pot with the bones. Add the tomato paste, parsley, bay leaves, peppercorns, and ½ teaspoon salt to the pot. Add enough water just to cover. Bring the stock to a gentle simmer, skimming any foam from the surface, and let simmer, gently, for 12 hours or overnight.

Strain the stock, discarding the solids, then place the stock back in the cleaned pot. Boil the stock until it is reduced to 1 gallon. Cool the stock completely then refrigerate or freeze until ready to use.

HEAVY BRINE

This brine is used for all sorts of applications, but mostly to get a subtle sweet-salty balance into thicker cuts and parts. For instance, we use it for brining our Smoked Pork Loin (page 32) and the tendons for our Nervetti Salad (page 83). Make a large batch, even if you don't need it all at once. The brine keeps in sealed containers at room temperature for weeks.

MAKES 1 GALLON

1 gallon water

1 cup brown sugar or Grade B maple syrup

1 head garlic, halved

A few black peppercorns

2 bay leaves

A few allspice berries

1 or 2 dried cloves

Fine sea salt

Combine the water, sugar, garlic, peppercorns, bay leaves, allspice, cloves, and ⅓ cup salt in a large pot, then bring to a boil. Remove from the heat and let the brine cool completely before using.

INDEX

Note: Page numbers in *italics* indicate photos on pages separate from recipes.

D

E

BLP

BURGESS LEA PRESS
NEW HOPE, PENNSYLVANIA

An affiliate of Running Press Book Publishers

Burgess Lea Press donates 100% of our after-tax profits on each book to culinary education, feeding the hungry, farmland preservation and other food-related causes.

www.burgessleapress.com

1 2 3 4 5 6 7 8 9 10

Printed in China by 1010 Printing Group Limited

Art direction by Ken Newbaker
Book design by Jan Derevjanik
Photography by Guy Ambrosino
Food styling by Kate Winslow
Design direction by Whitney Cookman
Book production by Victor Cataldo

ISBN: 978-1-941868-09-6
Library of Congress control number on file with the publisher